HOW·TO·BE
Happily
Employed
IN
DALLAS-FORT WORTH

HOW·TO·BE
Happily
Employed
IN
DALLAS-FORT WORTH

A Step-by-Step Guide to Finding the Job That's Right for You

BARBARA BLOCK &
JANICE BENJAMIN
WITH KATHRYN JONES

RANDOM HOUSE
New York

ACKNOWLEDGMENTS

We want to thank our respective families for their patience and support: Melissa, Julie and Anna; Bert, Brett and Blair. Also Steve Hermes for his original artwork direction.

Barbara Block and Janice Benjamin

I wish to acknowledge career consultants Mary Holdcroft, Taunee Besson and Ruth Glover for their help and advice.

I also wish to thank Abigail Davis for providing research assistance and Lisa Smith for the locator map of the Dallas–Fort Worth area.

Kathryn Jones

Copyright © 1990 by Barbara Block and Janice Benjamin

All rights reserved under the International and Pan-American Copyright Conventions. Published in the United States by Random House, Inc., New York, and simultaneously in Canada by Random House of Canada Limited, Toronto.

Library of Congress Cataloging-in-Publication Data

Block, Barbara.
    How to be happily employed n Dallas–Fort Worth: a step-by-step guide to finding the job that's right for you / by Barbara Block and Janice Benjamin.
        p.   cm.
    Includes bibliographical references.
    ISBN 0-679-73070-2
    1. Job hunting—Texas—Dallas. 2. Job hunting—Texas—Fort Worth.
    I. Benjamin, Janice. II. Title.
    HF5382.75.U62D353   1990
    650.14'09764'2812—dc20   89-37061

Manufactured in the United States of America
Book design by Charlotte Staub

9 8 7 6 5 4 3 2
First edition

CONTENTS

INTRODUCTION

Looking for work can be grueling. We understand. For the past fifteen years we have helped people figure out what they want to do and then have taught them how to find a job and determine a career plan.

We have learned a lot in those years that we'd like to share with you. We want to show you that by following a methodical, step-by-step procedure, you can minimize the fear and confusion while making the task of job hunting not only manageable but even enjoyable. With the right preparation, anyone who wants to can become happily employed.

"Just a minute!" you exclaim, remembering what a jungle it is out there. "I am not sure I can even find a job, let alone a good one. I will just stay where I am or take what I can get."

Wait! Before you close this book, let's look at a few facts from the U.S. Department of Labor.

FACT: Almost 120 million Americans are working.

FACT: Six to eight percent unemployment also means at least ninety-two percent of the population has a job.

Now, consider how most people find jobs:

- 6 percent through private employment agencies;

- 6 percent through public agencies;
- 17 percent through ads;
- 34 percent through friends, associates, and relatives;
- 30 percent through employers directly;
- 3 percent through school placement offices;
- 4 percent through trade union hiring and other methods.

What does this tell you? Most jobs (64 percent) are found through *direct contact* with friends, relatives, or the person doing the hiring.

What this adds up to is:

- There *are* jobs.
- The majority of openings are discovered through an individual's own networking efforts.
- The key to success is knowing what you want and having a systematic, organized, and informed approach to getting it.

So, while the bad news is that millions of people are looking for jobs right now, the good news, for you, is that most of them have no idea what they are doing.

We want you to be one of the few job hunters who know what they're doing. We have designed a procedure to lift you above the crowd, in order to land you a job.

This book is designed in two parts to give you everything you will need for your job search. The first part covers the job hunt. It will guide you through self-assessment exercises to help you focus and give you a comprehensive strategy for finding a job and getting hired. The second part of the book is a Resource Guide. We have compiled lists of local sources to contact. These include employers, organizations, publications, networks, and referral centers.

We believe you will benefit from this book if you fit any of the following categories:

- contemplating the possibility of making a change but not sure where to start;
- mildly curious as to whether you will learn anything new about job hunting and career changing;
- desperately looking for a job;

- wanting to help someone who is in transition;
- currently satisfied with your work but would like to be prepared just in case;
- well read on the subject of job hunting and confused as ever;
- not quite sure why you picked up this book but are experiencing the following:

tiredness, loss of energy	limited concentration span
detachment from people and events	psychosomatic complaints
irritability	depression, disorientation
emotional flare-ups	vague discontent with what once was important
boredom, cynicism, questioning of life	
feeling unappreciated	

In other words, this book is for anyone who sincerely wants to become happily employed. By following its approach, you will discover that what may seem an immense and discouraging effort can become an exciting adventure. Job hunting can provide an opportunity to change and grow, to go places and meet people you never knew existed, to learn about yourself and your capabilities, and to discover you can do things you never dreamed possible, or considered only dreams.

What's more, reading this book will give you a distinct advantage in today's labor market. Job hunting and career planning are considerably more complex and confusing than they used to be. Looking around: the world you see is a lot different from the one your parents knew. Typically, Dad worked in one company all his life, steadily moving up the ladder, retiring at age sixty-five. Mom, traditionally, stayed home and kept house. That is certainly not the job picture of today.

Instead, there is fierce global competition, burgeoning technological advancement, an unpredictable economy, a rash of mergers and corporate restructuring, a dramatic increase in the number of women and immigrants entering the workplace, and an equally dramatic number of workers being laid off or taking early retirement.

These trends will have a significant impact on your career.

- **There is no such thing as job security anymore.** The only security you have is knowing you can market yourself. Even if you don't want a new job right now, it is critical that you plan ahead in your career and be prepared for changes.

- **Getting ahead no longer means moving up.** Most companies have streamlined operations. There are fewer positions the higher you go. To advance in your career, you need to be open to other options—like lateral moves within the organization or out of it—or know how to make your current job more satisfying.

- **You have more options than ever before.** More and more employees are working flexible hours, sharing jobs, setting up work stations in their homes, retiring early, developing "composite careers" (earning a living from multiple sources of income), and, altogether, creating alternative careers and life-styles.

- **Most job openings will be in smaller businesses.** According to the data compiled by Dun & Bradstreet, 66 percent of all hiring occurs in firms with fewer than twenty employees; 80 percent of new jobs are being created in businesses less than four years old. Though they are more plentiful, jobs in small, emerging firms can be harder to find.

There is a lot to consider when you are planning a career. To help you, we have sifted through the mass of current literature, weeded out the redundant or irrelevant, and boiled the rest down to the most basic ingredients. We have tested the exercises and techniques in this book with hundreds of clients and they have proven highly successful. We have sought out the most helpful local sources and come up with alternative ideas in our effort to provide you with an easy-to-read, concise, and comprehensive job-hunting guide.

These pages can be quickly scanned or slowly pondered. You may follow each chapter sequentially or refer only to the sections that fit your needs. Specific steps and exercises are presented to take you from uncertainty, through the focusing, until you find an opening, get hired, and negotiate a salary. In addition, strategies are recommended to help you succeed in your new position as well as negotiate a raise. Should you desire a more detailed treatment of any topic, consult the Suggested Reading list at the back of the book.

If you want help finding what's "out there," industries to which you could transfer your skills, or places you can go for assistance, the Resource Guide tells you what your city has to offer and where to find it. Specific places and sources of information, complete with addresses, phone numbers, and descriptions are featured.

Our hope is that after working with this book, you will have the techniques to make things happen rather than waiting for them to happen.

Perhaps you will end up with what you knew you always wanted, or perhaps you will venture into unexpected territory. Whatever you decide, you will travel with the assurance and conviction that accompanies a well-thought-out decision.

HOW·TO·BE
Happily
Employed
IN
DALLAS-FORT WORTH

1
THE JOB SEARCH PROCESS:
A Basic Overview

You will learn that dead ends need not stop you.

A step-by-step process is the most efficient way to find a job. This chapter provides an overview or map of what those steps are. Then, in the following chapters, each step is described in detail.

The process is simple—and it works—but it probably won't be easy. In the search for your next job, you will likely encounter some false starts, wrong turns, and blind alleys. But don't let dead ends stop you. This book will show you how to return to a previous step, regroup, and proceed from there. Sometimes you may feel that you are back at the beginning. You will not, however, be starting from scratch. You will have made enormous progress by eliminating what you know you don't want or what doesn't work. In other words, when you follow this map, you may get waylaid but you won't be lost for long.

Examine the list of steps now. Review it when you've finished reading the whole book. And use it as a guideline throughout your job search.

PHASE I: IDENTIFYING THE JOB YOU WANT

- **Start.** You are confused and unsure. What do you want to do? Where do you start? What's next? You probably long for the security of a well-defined job and detest the uncertainty of not knowing what is around the next corner.

- **Focus.** With pen and paper in hand, do the exercises in this book and create a detailed checklist of what you want and need in a job.
- **Develop a job description.** Using your checklist, create a brief description of the job you are seeking.

Now that you have some direction, it is time to find job titles that fit your description.

PHASE II: JOB RESEARCH AND NETWORKING

- **Informally interview.** Friends and family help you refine your job objective and expand your network.
- **Interview for information.** Talk to professionals to learn more about the specific job/industry/company in which you are interested.
- **Join** relevant professional organizations, where possible.
- **Look** at trade and business directories and publications in the library.
- **Read** newspapers and periodicals. Write to specific companies for their literature.
- **Explore** more than one field. See if your ideal job description matches other jobs in different industries.

PHASE III: GETTING HIRED

- **Apply for a job.** Recontact people to discuss employment.
- **Cover all bases: want ads, agencies, and other intermediaries.** Let the time you devote to each job search activity be proportional to the likely payoff. (Remember, most of the best jobs are never advertised.)

- **Interview for jobs.** Get lots of practice. It takes a string of "nos" to get the "yes"!
- **Consider taking a survival job to fund your job search campaign.** It may or may not be a stepping-stone in your career path.
- **Keep at it with dogged persistence and be positive.** You *will* become "happily employed."

2
PIECING TOGETHER THE PUZZLE

Before you grab your hat and coat and dash
out the door to the nearest job interview,
you need to take some time to reflect.

There are two approaches to job hunting. One is what
we call the *shotgun approach*. You're probably familiar
with this one, since it is the tack most people take.

It goes something like this: you're desperate to find
a job, so you comb the Sunday want ads, send out 765
resumes, knock on every personnel door within three
hundred miles, and pray. When someone asks you what
kind of work you're looking for, you generally answer
"Anything!" (hoping to keep all fronts covered), or
something vague like "Computers . . ." (because Uncle
Fred said computers was a growing field), and then you
add, "but I'm open to anything." Time passes. Rejec-
tions pile up. Your energy, optimism, and confidence
plummet. Things look pretty bleak.

Suddenly, luck strikes. The Jolly Janitorial Service
needs a bookkeeper. Of course, that isn't quite what
you had in mind (not that you really had anything in
mind except ending the anxiety of being unemployed).
But at this point, anything looks good. You apply for
the job and get it. Time to celebrate, right? Not yet.

Within a month you begin to grow restless. But you
can't just quit. How would it look on your resume? So
you stick it out. You drag yourself to work in the morning, watch the seconds tick by on the clock, and dream
about becoming a beach bum in Tahiti. You resign

yourself to the fact that before too long you will be right back in the cold, cruel world of job hunting again. It's either that or stay at Jolly Janitorial forever.

And so it goes, day after day, until one morning you realize you have got to get another job—fast. And you begin the shotgun cycle all over again.

A BETTER WAY

Another approach to finding a job is the one we call *focusing*. Before you grab your hat and coat and dash out the door to the nearest job interview, take some time to reflect. Look within yourself and ask some questions. What could spark your enthusiasm and send you flying out of bed in the morning? What would bring you a feeling of fulfillment and satisfaction? What, specifically, are your skills, interests, and needs?

The process is similar to putting together a jigsaw puzzle. If you don't get all the pieces out of the box, you're going to have a tough time completing the picture. In the same way, if you don't uncover parts of yourself that may have been hidden up to now, you'll be unable to form a clear picture of the job that's right for you. These hidden parts include your needs, values, interests, and skills. They must be clearly identified and evaluated before you can reach your career goal.

THE PROCESS

How do you delve in and come up with all this information about yourself?

One way is simply to ask yourself questions: What am I good at doing? What do I need and value? What do I enjoy? What motivates me? Usually, though, this method doesn't work very well. It is difficult for many of us to take stock of ourselves accurately and objectively. Our self-perceptions have been warped. Self-doubt distorts our judgment.

Fortunately, however, tools in the form of questionnaires and inventories are available to aid in our self-evaluation. These range from simple list-making techniques to sophisticated computer-scored instruments like the Strong Vocational Interest Inventory. But whatever their level of sophistication, these tools do not operate like slot machines. You can't just enter the data like so many coins and expect your ideal job to be revealed. Nothing—no test, no exercise—will do that for you. There are no magic solutions. There are no crystal balls. These tools are more like mirrors offering you a reflection of who you are, but you must see and understand what is being reflected before you can use it.

At the end of this chapter you will find a series of exercises that we have used successfully with hundreds of clients to help them focus and clarify their direction. Take the time to do these exercises. By thinking through your responses, playing with the information, and analyzing the results, you allow ideas and possibilities to take shape.

THE PROCEDURE

When we work with clients, we schedule one-hour sessions twice a week for three weeks to discuss and interpret the exercises they do at home. Structure, routine, organization, and discipline in completing the exercises are not only helpful, they are vital. Set up your own schedule for devoting time to self-assessment.

1. Set aside periods of uninterrupted time, perhaps ninety minutes, three times a week, to do the exercises, and read this book. Stick to this schedule rigorously.
2. Create a private work space.
3. Keep all your written work in a folder or notebook. Avoid scattering pieces of information all over the place. You probably feel fragmented enough already. We give our clients folders with side pockets. You will need a similar system for keeping track of records and information.
4. Keep a small pocket notebook with you at all times to jot down names, observations, "aha!" experiences, and stray ideas.

5. Save receipts. If you are seeking employment in the same trade or business, you can deduct your job-hunting expenses. Be sure to ask your accountant about this.
6. Discuss your progress with someone supportive. Great ideas often surface during conversations.
7. Keep a journal. Writing can be therapeutic as well as inspirational.

THE OUTCOME

It is through such techniques that you will come up with a checklist of what you want and need in a job. This checklist becomes the criteria by which you will evaluate your choices and make decisions. The idea is to find a job that closely matches your checklist and meshes well with your identity and abilities—the major prerequisite for being happily employed.

Let's take an example. Say that after completing the exercises and analyzing the results, certain factors stand out as important to you:

1. You prefer to be highly visible in the workplace and to have authority over others.
2. You are good at planning projects and instructing and motivating people.
3. You want decision-making responsibility.
4. You are interested in the financial world and would like to work for a large organization.
5. You would love your own office but want to work in a team atmosphere.

You may object that you already know these things about yourself. However, experience has taught us that unless such preferences are written down, they usually remain muddled in your head and therefore easily forgotten and essentially useless.

By writing down your personal job criteria, what may seem like random bits and pieces of self-awareness will begin to form the skeleton of a job description. And by fleshing out this list, then organizing it into a few sentences, you will be able to describe what you want in a job clearly and briefly.

For example, one possible job description based on the previous list of preferences might be: "I am looking for a management position in a financial institution, perhaps a bank, where I can use my skills in planning, training, and human resource development." (Notice that you need not come up with a specific job title at this point. What you want is a brief summary of what you'd like to do.)

By the end of this chapter you should be able to shape your checklist into a clear, crisp job description. As you do your research, you may find that your description fits a number of job titles, or that your goals will change. Discovery and change are important elements in this process.

Even if you are convinced from the beginning that you want to be a tree surgeon, we urge you to keep an open mind. There are many exciting and lucrative possibilities that are unknown to you at this moment but may be a wonderful fit.

If you keep your options open, you won't get stuck. If you reach a dead end, which often happens in a job search, you'll have alternative routes. For example, what happens if you discover that there are no job openings for tree surgeons? Not to worry. Through scrupulous investigation you have found another field where you can work with your hands, clipping and trimming, creating new shapes, and restoring damaged roots. You become a hairdresser.

This may be a silly example, but it illustrates an important point. Without contingency plans, you risk terminal discouragement on the first time out. With a number of options open—the number limited by your imagination alone—you'll have plenty of leads to follow when that first disappointment occurs. But without focusing on your ultimate goal, the options you choose might fail to match your personal criteria. Thus, the focusing process enables you to hold fast to your objective while simultaneously broadening your scope.

One of our clients, Margie, came to us bored with her administrative job. After evaluating her work, leisure,

10

and community activities, she realized she needed to be in a more creative position, using her skills in researching, organizing, and analyzing information, and communicating her conclusions both verbally and on paper. She talked with friends about these discoveries. They gave her ideas about where to look, who to contact, and associations to join. Within five months, she took a job selling advertising for a local magazine, not to meet her original objective but only as a stepping-stone to the more creative side of marketing. She made valuable contacts, got excellent advice, learned the lingo, and was able to develop a sharper focus in a particular area of interest. Nine months later, she was hired by a small advertising firm as a market researcher. This job matched her criteria perfectly, though she had never even heard of such a position before beginning her exploration.

This example not only demonstrates the value of focusing but also suggests that there are many routes to a goal—very few are straight, short, and precise. The important considerations are that your goals be clear and your efforts compatible with them.

BENEFITS

Even if you firmly believe that you know precisely what you want, we urge you to do the focusing exercises. At the very least, you will find them reassuring. By going through these steps now, you will be preparing yourself for the hiring interview, where you will be asked such tricky questions as "Tell me about yourself," "What are your major strengths and weaknesses?" or "Why do you want this job?"

But by far the most dramatic benefit of focusing is an amazing phenomenon called synchronicity. In synchronicity, your intentions, like a magnet, seem to attract people and opportunities that support your efforts and propel you toward your goals. We tell our clients to expect coincidences as their objectives become more concrete.

Another very important psychological benefit of focusing is its stabilizing effect. No doubt you have noticed that job hunting puts you on an emotional roller coaster. Some days you're surging with optimism and enthusiasm. Other days you're overwhelmed by negativity and despair. If you have a checklist and a goal, if you are disciplined and organized, if you feel clear in your own mind about your direction, you are better able to cope with the ups and downs. Focused job hunting feels a little like being caught in quicksand but knowing there's a bottom. It is not comfortable, but at least you know it won't pull you down for good.

Still, periods of doubt, fear, and confusion are a normal, even essential, part of the job-hunting process. No amount of preparation is going to eliminate the discomfort completely. Like focusing with the lens of a camera, you need to go through the blur to get a vivid picture. The point is not to fight the confusion. Let yourself go through it. If you are unable to cope with the chaos and become bogged down by negativity, we strongly urge you to seek counseling.

We know from experience that careful self-assessment combined with the practical steps and the local resources described in the following section will produce positive results. Stay with it. When the fog clears and you're doing the work you love, the world will look a lot brighter.

FOCUSING EXERCISES

The following individual exercises should be done in order. By the time you come to the end of this section, all the information will be clustered, summarized, and used to help you arrive at a job description that is custom-designed for you.

Exercise 1
PERSONAL PROFILE

This exercise will give you a wealth of information about yourself. The first thing to do is to divide your age into thirds. If you are 42, then you will come up with these three age groups: 1–14, 14–28, 28–42.

Now, relax and let your thoughts drift back. Start to recall some of your past accomplishments, the things you did well, enjoyed doing, and felt good about, regardless of what others thought. These experiences must be something *you* did, not those you watched your friends doing. They may have made big splashes or just tiny, quiet ripples. For example: learning to tie your shoes, reupholstering a chair, finding a job, writing a poem, solving a problem, planning a party for four or a banquet for four hundred. The important thing here is that *you felt good about the activity, enjoyed doing it, and did it well.*

Try to come up with at least three achievements for each of your three age groups—that will give you at least nine achievements in all. This may take a few minutes or may require a few days. Don't force anything—just pay attention to whatever surfaces. If nothing comes to mind, that's all right. Give it time. Sleep on it. Perhaps you are being overly critical, or trying too hard to find just the right experience. This exercise will work best if you don't try to influence the outcome, if you're willing to take what pops up.

The following chart shows you what to do once you have recalled nine experiences. The chart is divided into three columns. In the first column, put your age at the time of the experience. In the second column, describe in detail exactly what you did to accomplish the experience. Write a little story about it. And in the third column, write down the reason it was a success for you. For example, you and a friend may have both made paper hats when you were five years old. But for you, it was doing it on your own that made it a success. (For your friend, it may have been receiving compliments.)

Age	Description	Reason
5	My sister gave me the idea to make paper doily hats. Together we collected material scraps, yarn, and bits of paper from around the house, glued them on, and I made about a dozen different designs. We hung them on the wall like in a store and made up a story about a gallery of hats to tell to whomever would listen.	My parents and friends complimented me.
8	My family took a trip to Colorado and took a lot of pictures which I spent a day arranging on construction paper. Then I put the pages into an album and found things about Colorado in an encyclopedia to include too. I took the album to school for sharing day and was complimented by my teacher who put it on display in the hall showcase.	I was recognized for something I created.
10	I gave a speech in class on my favorite food, potato chips, and how they're made. I had persuaded Mom to take me through a potato chip factory to see how they were made. I took pictures at the factory and glued them onto a posterboard to take to class. My teacher gave me an A on the speech because I had spent so much time learning about potato chips and had used good visual aids.	I was recognized for working hard at learning something new.
12	I thought it would be neat for the YMCA camp I went to to have a yearbook for everyone to take home. The Directors liked my idea and agreed to help. I asked the campers to write about what they liked best about camp and interviewed the Staff about the camp's history. It was such a success that the Staff used it to tell parents about sending their kids to camp.	I had created something that was well-accepted by others and was used even after that camp year had ended.
15	My mom and her friend decided to start a catering business. I over-heard them talking about what to call their business, so I looked for names by flipping through magazines, scanning the phone book, and talking with friends. I came up with "PARTY PALS" and my mom and her friend loved it. Mom get a lot of pleasure from telling people that her daughter had created the name.	Mom recognized me for my interest and creativity. I liked being the creator of something that had visibility.

19	A good friend who was a college reporter asked me for help in writing a story on the history of the community college. I started out just gathering information as background material from newspaper clippings and ended up doing the whole thing for him. It appeared on the front page and everyone at the school complimented me. I felt like a celebrity.	I was recognized for my abilities. I liked the celebrity status.
24	I was appointed to head a task force for the Professional Administrators Association I belonged to. Our job was to develop a report on new ways of networking for women that would be presented to the National Convention. I co-authored the report and then presented it at the convention. In the audience was a reporter from a national women's magazine, and she asked to publish the report.	As part of a team, I was able to complete a project and was recognized for my efforts.
26	I was administrative assistant to the President of a safety equipment firm. After looking through trade journals, I noticed that the firms ads looked dull and uninteresting. One day I found a diplomatic way to mention it to our boss. His response was to come up with some suggested plans for improving our advertising. I met with the Marketing Director and we began talking about our need to make some changes. He asked me to contact a couple of local agencies to come in and meet with him for the purpose of creating a new campaign.	I took a risk and was rewarded for it.

Exercise 2
PERSONAL PROFILE ANALYSIS

Now is the time to analyze the Personal Profile Chart you completed in Exercise 1. If you examine the stories, you will see a pattern emerge; the same skills, values, relationships, rewards, and interests are repeated over and over again. This is called your *motivating pattern*. It is what "turns you on," gets you going, and keeps you stimulated.

Every motivating pattern has four ingredients: a recurring way of relating to others; a group of five to seven skills; a favorite subject matter; and, most noteworthy, one motivational thrust of critical importance.

Put these ingredients together and you can see what is missing in your current job, or what you need to have in your next position. For example, you may learn that you are motivated by risk-taking, adventurous situations, or encouraging and supporting others. If you spend your day bent over a computer, you can start to see why you're miserable and what changes you need to make to become happily employed.

Here is what you need to do to discover your motivating pattern. Reread each of the stories you wrote about your achievements. While you read them, ask yourself these questions:

1. What skills and abilities do I use to bring about this achievement (see the skill list on pages 23–24)?
2. What do I show an interest in (numbers, things, people, ideas, words)?
3. How do I interact with people? What roles do I play (alone, on a team, as the boss, as a teacher)?
4. What do I get out of this achievement? What does this show I need to give me satisfaction (excelling, building something, acquiring things, getting results, creating a product, recognition)?

Using the sample analysis chart on the next page as a guideline, make a chart and record your own answers.

PERSONAL PROFILE ANALYSIS

Achievement	Personality Skills	Transferable Skills/Special Knowledge	Special Interests	Interaction Style/Roles	Needs/Values
#1 Paper hats	creative resourceful artistic	assemble materials develop ideas design	working with objects and things of art	working with another	recognition to be creative
#2 Trip album	creative initiative motivated	organize information arrange materials research	learning about new places	independent	recognition to be creative
#3 Speech on potato chips	resourceful initiative industrious original	present information verbally & visually research explain a process	researching and organizing new information in a creative way	independent with others	to work hard to accomplish a task recognition
#4 Summer camp	innovative ambitious assertive	influence others build a team coordinate a project lead others	researching & organizing information for presentation to others	a leader	authority recognition to be innovative
#5 Catering business	initiative original helpful	identify need investigate create	creative projects	independent a consultant an originator	recognition to be creative to be helpful to others to be visible
#6 Write a story	resourceful reliable motivated	research organize interview journalistic writing	historical research	independent a colleague	to be visible peer recognition
#7 Head of task force	goal-directedness self-confident verbal	develop report delegate tasks analyze information write public speaking	working for the benefit of women's issues	a leader a team player an idea developer	achievement to be part of a team effort–affiliation influence authority
#8 Administrative assistant at the safety firm	assertive resourceful creative motivated	identify a need consult create recommend	advertising/ marketing	independent a consultant	responsibility – authority acceptance of ideas competency

Exercise 3
VALUES INVENTORY

Values are what give meaning and purpose to life. They are vital to happiness and satisfaction—including happiness and satisfaction on a job. Even if you think that you already understand your own values, it will be helpful to identify and evaluate them when making a career decision. Rate them as to the degree of satisfaction they give you, using the following scale. Base your reaction on your first gut-level response. What you learn will be used in later exercises.

1—Not very important
2—Somewhat important
3—Important and would like to have in my life
4—Very important, critical to include in my choices

____**Aesthetics:** appreciate study, enjoy beauty of things and ideas

____**Appearance:** concern for one's own attractiveness or that of surroundings

____**Adventure:** activities which involve risk, excitement, and unpredictable results

____**Authority:** control over the activities or destiny of others, power

____**Affiliation:** to be recognized part of the group

____**Broad-mindedness:** open-minded, tolerant, concern for equality

____**Competency:** to be capable and effective

____**Community:** live in location which fits life-style where one can get involved in community affairs

____**Competition:** engage in activities which pit abilities against others

____**Creativity:** be innovative, imaginative, create something new

____**Friendship:** develop close relationships with others

____**Family:** being with family members

____**Fast Pace:** high activity, work done rapidly

____**Health:** freedom from disease, pain, stress, and suffering

____**Helping Others:** work for the benefit of others

____**Honesty:** truthful, sincere

____**Independence:** do things on own without a lot of orders and direction from others

____**Influence:** be in position to change attitudes or opinions of others

____**Intellectual Status:** acknowledged as an expert, possessing intellectual prowess

____**Leisure:** time for enjoyment, pleasure, and relaxation

____**Love:** devotion, warm attachment, and taking care of loved ones

____**Material Status:** possessing financial or material possessions

____**Moral Fulfillment:** contribute to set of moral standards

____**Order:** neatness, organization, planning

____**Peace:** a world free of conflict and war

____**Religious Faith:** obedience to and activity in behalf of Supreme Being

____**Recognition:** getting respect, approval, prestige for what you do

____**Security:** assured of keeping job, free from concern of loss of resources

____**Self-Expression:** use of natural talents or abilities which express who you are

____**Wisdom:** mature understanding of life, good sense, and insight

____If you can think of any others, please add.

List below all the values you rated no. 4.

_____   _____   _____

_____   _____   _____

_____   _____   _____

_____   _____   _____

_____   _____   _____

Of the top five which is the very most important to you? Then second most important, etc.

1._____   3._____   5._____

2._____   4._____

FEEDBACK SHEET

Feedback from other people is a very valuable, but often neglected, tool in making career decisions. The following technique is an easy and enjoyable way to get it.

Make four copies of this sheet. Give a copy to friends, business associates, family, or anyone with whom you would feel comfortable doing this. Ask them to fill out this form—as honestly and objectively as they can. Don't look over their shoulders while they are working, but you may discuss their comments afterward. You may want to mail one or two Feedback Sheets to friends with a self-addrssed stamped envelope and a request that they be returned within a few days.

Choose a variety of individuals whom you know in different ways. You may not agree with every assessment, and, indeed, some people's observations may be biased by their own needs and values. That is why we recommend giving the Feedback Sheet to at least four people.

FEEDBACK SHEET

1. What do you see as my major personality strengths?

2. What do you see as my most marketable skills?

3. What kind of environment do you see me working in?

4. What do you think I need in a job?

5. What do you see in me that I probably don't see in myself?

Exercise 5
SKILL IDENTIFICATION AND CLUSTERING

Most of us have difficulty identifying our skills. We tend to lump them all together and dismiss certain ones, thinking, "Anyone can do that"; or we completely overlook some of our most important assets.

Perhaps it would help to look at skills as falling into three categories. Examine the following lists and underline the skills you have or would like to develop.

PERSONALITY SKILLS (Otherwise known as self-management skills, or even "personality traits," since we rarely think of them as skills). To get in touch with your personality skills, ask yourself: What personal characteristics do I have? Here are some examples:

academic	congenial	formal	moderate
accurate	conscientious	frank	modest
active	conservative	friendly	motivated
adaptable	considerate	generous	obliging
adventurous	consistent	good-	open-
aggressive	cooperative	natured	minded
alert	courageous	healthy	opportu-
ambitious	curious	helpful	nistic
analytical	deliberate	humorous	optimistic
artistic	dependable	imaginative	organized
bold	determined	independent	patient
broad-	dignified	industrious	persistent
minded	discreet	informal	pleasant
calm	dominant	intellectual	poised
capable	eager	intelligent	polite
careful	easygoing	introspective	practical
cautious	efficient	inventive	precise
cheerful	energetic	kind	progressive
clear-	fair-minded	logical	prudent
thinking	far-sighted	loving	punctual
clever	firm	loyal	purposeful
competent	flexible	mature	quick
competitive	forceful	methodical	quiet
confident	forgiving	meticulous	rational

realistic	sensible	steady	trusting
relaxed	sensitive	strong	trustworthy
reliable	serious	supportive	unassuming
resourceful	sharp-	tactful	understanding
responsible	witted	tenacious	verbal
self-	sincere	thorough	versatile
confident	sociable	thoughtful	warm
self-	spontaneous	tolerant	wise
controlled	stable	tough	witty

SPECIAL KNOWLEDGE SKILLS (also called work/ activity skills). These are more technical skills that relate to a particular field, job, or subject matter. They involve learning and memory. To get in touch with your special knowledge, look at what you do every day in your job and your free time. Here are some examples out of an almost endless list of possibilities:

computer programming
planning trips
being a chemist
operating a mainframe
  computer
typing legal documents
tailoring suits
preparing a lesson plan
repairing a car

statistical analysis
fluency in French
charitable fund-raising
magazine layout
coaching volleyball
sales training
lobbying for labor
  reform
graphic design

Jot down some special knowledge skills that you have:

TRANSFERABLE SKILLS. You use these skills to deal with data, people, or things. They can be used in a variety of settings and fields. For example, a high school teacher could transfer his teaching skills to a corporate training department. To get in touch with your transferable skills, look at the following action words and think about which ones apply to you that could be transferred from one job to another.

achieve	counsel	integrate	propose
act	coach	interpret	publicize
adapt	create	interview	publish
administer	decide	invent	reconcile
advertise	define	investigate	recruit
advise	delegate	lead	research
analyze	design	liaison	resolve
anticipate	develop	manage	revise
arrange	edit	market	schedule
assemble	enlist	mediate	select
assess	empower	merchandise	speak
assist	evaluate	moderate	stimulate
budget	facilitate	negotiate	summarize
build	forecast	operate	supervise
calculate	fund-raise	organize	survey
collaborate	govern	perform	synthesize
communicate	hire	persuade	systematize
conceptual-	index	plan	teach
ize	influence	problem-	team build
consult	inform	solve	write
coordinate	initiate	promote	

Exercise 6
CLUSTERING YOUR SKILLS

In this exercise, you will start grouping and summarizing your skills. First, go back to the Personal Profile Analysis, in Exercise 2. Look at the skills you noted in columns 2 and 3. These reflect the skills you enjoyed using in the past. Bear in mind that just because you can do something doesn't mean you like to do it. To become "happily employed," you should focus on the skills that give you pleasure.

Next, turn to the three categories of skills listed on pages 20–22. Look at the skills you underlined that may not have shown up in your achievements but which you have displayed or would like to develop.

Finally, refer to the Feedback Sheets. Look at the skills other people feel you have.

Take the skills you identified in each of these three exercises and group them under the categories provided on page 25. You will find that some skills will fit into several clusters (e.g., "can communicate with management" could fall under managerial as well as verbal communication). If you cannot decide which cluster to include the skill under, list it under both. Don't worry about being perfect—just do it.

Here are some examples of the individual skills you might list under each category:

LEADERSHIP
lead, motivate, enthusiastic, sociable, leading marketing professionals

MANAGERIAL
organize, implement, interview, understand management by objectives, supervisory skills, supportive, tenacious, manage a computer software distribution center

TEACHING/TRAINING
design, influence,
motivate others

VERBAL COMMUNICATION
able to communicate
concepts, public
speaking, technical
training

WRITING/EDITING
write newsletters,
organize, original

OFFICE/MANUAL SKILLS
operate office equipment,
problem-solve

PHYSICAL/OUTDOOR
coach volleyball,
adventurous, team build

RESEARCH/ANALYSIS
resourceful, develop
ideas, thorough, expert
in zoology

ARTISTIC/ PERFORMING
graphic design,
innovative, courageous,
public speaking

SOCIAL/ INTERPERSONAL
counsel individuals,
sharp-witted, interview
skills

SCIENTIFIC/ MATHEMATICAL
knowledge of statistics,
punctual, conceptual,
pharmaceutical
manufacturing
technology

SALES/PROMOTIONAL/ FUND-RAISING
marketing analysis,
ambitious, bold, conduct
a survey, radio sales
experience

ADVOCACY
facilitate, idealistic,
manipulate, implement,
knowledge of child care
legislation, mediation

OTHER (any categories
you can think of not on
this page)

Now, on the following chart, cluster your own skills:

SAMPLE FORM
CLUSTERING YOUR SKILLS

Leadership

_____
_____
_____

Managerial

_____
_____
_____

Teaching/Training

_____
_____
_____

Verbal Communication

_____
_____
_____

Writing/Editing

_____
_____
_____

Office/Manual Skills

_____
_____
_____

Physical/Outdoor

_____
_____
_____

Research/Analysis

_____
_____
_____

Artistic/Performing

_____
_____
_____

Social/Interpersonal

_____
_____
_____

**Scientific/
Mathematical**

_____
_____
_____

**Sales/Promotional/
Fund-Raising**

_____
_____
_____

Advocacy

_____
_____
_____

Your Own Cluster

_____
_____
_____

Exercise 7
MAGIC WAND I

Now it is time to really have fun. In order for this exercise to be effective, you must be totally fanciful and even a little crazy!

We're going to give you a magic wand. If, with a flick of the stick, you could have anything you wanted in a job, what would you include? Make a "grocery list" below of everything you would ideally love to have in your work. Don't try to be realistic—that comes later. Right now just put down what you would like to have in your dream job. When you can't think of what else you'd like, list everything you know you would *definitely not* want.

Example: Money—$25,000 to $35,000
Travel—about eight to ten trips a year, even overseas
Opportunity to speak in public, preferably to large groups of over a hundred
Someday, have my own marketing firm
I definitely don't want strict nine-to-five hours
Don't want to share an office
Not a lot of routine and paperwork

Remember, you don't have to show this to anyone, nor will you necessarily ever convert all of this "wish list" into reality. The point is to have fun by writing down whatever comes to mind.

Exercise 8
MAGIC WAND II

You still have your magic wand. Now, from your "grocery list" of ideas, write a little story, a description of your ideal fantasy job. *Do not include a job title.*

Your fantasy job description represents your dream. Whether it now seems realistic or not, respect it because it reflects very real needs. There's a good chance its basic ingredients will be similar to those found in your Personal Profile Analysis.

Use these "dream criteria" to evaluate job choices. As you research employment opportunities, ask yourself, "How many of my criteria will be met in this job?" Of course, you will have to be realistic, set priorities, and sacrifice some of your needs for the sake of others. But, to be happily employed, you must never lose sight of your ideal job.

Example: I love to come up with new ideas. I want to conduct brainstorming sessions and head a team that pulls together a lot of resources to develop projects and events. But once I develop the project and get it going, I want to delegate it and let someone else run it. I really love dealing with environmental impact issues or anything to do with nature and animals. I'd also be interested in consulting on projects in the arts.

Exercise 9
SUMMARY SHEET

By now you have collected a lot of valuable information. You have examined your past achievements and identified skills, interests, values, and interactive styles. You have also analyzed your needs and values, clustered your skills, obtained feedback, and even taken a flight into fantasy with your magic wand.

Now what do you do with this mass of information? The chart below will help you pull everything together.

Take what you discovered in the previous exercises and anything else you know about yourself, and fill in each of the following sections with the appropriate information. Then circle one to three items in each category that have priority for you.

Here is an example of one job seeker's Summary Sheet. Your own sheet, of course, will reflect your particular situation:

NEEDS/VALUES	SHORT-/LONG-TERM GOALS	FINANCIAL NEEDS
1. Authority 2. Creativity 3. To be helpful 4. Work with others	1. Volunteer in environmental issues 2. Take marketing course 3. Own business—five years 4. Work on financial planning 5. Join Toastmasters International	1. $40,000 plus 2. Pension plan 3. Medical benefits 4. Start forced savings

WORKING ENVIRONMENT	INTERESTS	GEOGRAPHIC LOCATION	ROLES
1. Happy, supportive people 2. My own office 3. Lots of windows 4. Informal/ casual	1. Design programs 2. The environment 3. Animals 4. Events planning 5. Learning	1. East Coast 2. Close to home 3. In large city	1. Leader 2. Teacher 3. Collaborate 4. Team worker

SPECIAL KNOWLEDGE	TRANSFERABLE SKILLS	PERSONALITY SKILLS
1. Biology 2. Public speaking 3. Expertise in MacIntosh computers 4. Photography 5. Spanish	1. Manage 2. Teach 3. Project development 4. Generate ideas 5. Research	1. Analytical 2. Trustworthy 3. Innovative 4. Cooperative 5. Inspirational

Exercise 10
JOB DESCRIPTION I

This exercise helps you answer the question "What do you want to do?" Your answer can literally make or break your job search. Your response should be clear, concise, and to the point so that the person asking the question quickly understands what you are looking for and how she or he can best help you.

The answer to the question is, of course, your job description. Remember, you won't necessarily come up with a specific position, but you will have an objective which may match several job titles.

This worksheet will start you out by taking the information from the Summary Sheet, condensing it, and pulling out the key elements of a job description.

Begin by filling in the following statements. Don't try to be perfect. Just write down whatever you feel is right

I see that my major skill areas are ——————

————————————————————

My skills tend to be more related to

—— people —— data —— things

Perhaps some strengths and skills I may want to develop include ——————————

————————————————————

I see that my interests are ——————————

Perhaps I would like to develop the following interests:

————————————————————

————————————————————

I found that I like to interact with people by: ——

————————————————————

I learned that to be happy and fulfilled, I need _____

_____

I was surprised that _____

_____

I learned that I am motivated by _____

_____

Some ideas I have from doing this are _____

_____

Exercise 11
JOB DESCRIPTION II

We will now organize the information from Job Description I. Look back at what you wrote, then complete the following statements. Just write freely. Don't worry about what it sounds like now. You will polish it up later.

THE KIND OF POSITION OR ROLE YOU WANT (e.g., director, salesperson, coordinator, team member, manager, consultant):

USING THESE SKILLS (those strongest skills and abilities you have already identified):

IN THIS KIND OF ORGANIZATION (e.g., small, larger, nonprofit):

DEALING WITH THIS SUBJECT MATTER (e.g., financial management, ecology, employee relations, sales, computers):

DOING THESE KINDS OF ACTIVITIES (e.g., creating spread sheets, educating the public, designing training programs):

JOB DESCRIPTION III

Now it's time to begin to consolidate a job description. Start by writing in paragraph form everything you listed in Job Descriptions I and II. Your first attempts may feel awkward and too long. That's fine. You can rewrite several times until you're satisfied.

Here are some examples of job objectives:

SAMPLE JOB OBJECTIVE 1:

I am seeking a managerial position in a small company where I can use my skills in administration, training, and marketing to motivate sales staff and create new marketing strategies for increasing product visibility and sales.

SAMPLE JOB OBJECTIVE 2:

I am seeking a staff position in a community agency where I could integrate my skills in project coordination, volunteer supervision, and promotion to improve the community image of the agency and promote its causes.

Now create a paragraph of your own.

MY JOB OBJECTIVE:

And now you have it—a clear, focused description of the kind of job you want. It may change (and probably will), but you have discovered a direction and a starting point.

OTHER TOOLS FOR SELF-ASSESSMENT

To help you take more pieces of the puzzle out of the box, you may want to consider these additional self-assessment tools.

Testing and Analysis

Personality, aptitude, and vocational tests vary in format and degree of sophistication. Some are multiple choice, some are sentence completions, and others can be questionnaires. The majority of these tests have been designed to assess personality, interests, and aptitudes for a particular career.

Keep in mind that tests are merely indicators of vocational preference and should serve only to *reconfirm* the information gained through self-assessment. In other words, test results provide just a few more pieces of the puzzle; alone, they are not valid.

The standardized tests described here should always be administered and interpreted by a trained professional who is knowledgeable about the instruments' applications as well as limitations. Testing is available from a variety of career consultants, psychologists, and college placement and community centers. These are listed in the Resource Guide.

The *Strong-Campbell Interest Inventory* (SCII) is the most popular vocational test. Your interests are compared with those of satisfied workers in about ninety different occupations. Based on the degree of similarity or dissimilarity to them, it suggests possible occupations to explore.

The *Myers-Briggs Type Indicator* is a work preference indicator. This multiple-choice test suggests what types of people, environment, and activities you would find most compatible.

The *General Aptitude Test Battery* measures a range of aptitudes, such as verbal and numerical abilities, manual dexterity, and command of spatial relationships. This is a timed test usually given in a small group. The results are especially useful for vocational reentry and retraining.

The Tummy Grabber

We have found this to be a helpful tool for "visual" people. During the next four to six weeks, collect articles, pictures, ads, etc., that "grab" you. When anything you see, hear, or read piques your interest or causes you to react positively, tear it out or jot down a few words about it on a piece of paper and toss it in an envelope. Do *not* try to figure out why you chose this particular item, just collect the material.

At the end of four to six weeks, lay the material out on the floor and see what you have. You may be in for some surprises. Do you pick up any patterns? Do you see anything new popping out? Or does this serve to reinforce what you already suspected was your interest?

Begin today. Do not analyze—just put the material in an envelope and forget it until several weeks have passed.

3
INFORMAL
INTERVIEWING

When you know what you want and can
communicate your goals to others, you are
well on the way to becoming happily employed.

What if you have come up with a marvelous-sounding job description but have no idea what to call it? What if no such position exists as far as you know? Don't be concerned. The purpose of this chapter is to help you find job titles that fit your criteria. And, as a by-product, when you begin matching your goals to jobs in the outside world, you will clarify your objectives. Finally, in the process of clarification, you will be building and expanding your network. How? When you are able to clearly tell others what you are looking for, they will be able to link you up with people who can help you. This is called "networking." And since 64 percent of all jobs are found via the grapevine, networking is what job hunting is all about.

For some people, the thought of approaching others about a job has about as much appeal as walking barefoot through a field of broken glass. If you feel this way, give us a chance to convince you that networking for a job can be painless and even fun. You will find that if you are focused and proceed step-by-step, you can enjoy yourself while you're looking for work.

For convenience and ease, we have broken down the networking process into two phases. The first phase is what we call *informal interviewing*. In this phase, you talk to people you know—friends and family—to get information, advice, assistance, feedback, and support. Done correctly, this kind of interaction is a low-stress but highly effective entry into the job market.

Even if you have zeroed in on a job title, we encourage you to do the informal interviewing and leave yourself open to other possibilities. By clinging to the familiar, or by deciding too quickly, you may overlook exciting, fulfilling, and profitable alternatives to your original choice. Just because you have worked only as a teacher doesn't mean the word *teacher* is indelibly stamped on your forehead. Changing your professional identity is partly a matter of repackaging yourself. Informal interviewing is part of the repackaging process.

THE OUTCOME

Like a dress rehearsal before opening night, informal interviews allow you to practice without the pressure of having to perform perfectly. It's easier and wiser to test the waters with a friend than with a stranger who will decide your career fate. You will have a chance later to polish your presentation and further clarify your objective.

1. You'll become more focused, articulate, and confident each time you express your goal. In the beginning, especially if you are switching careers, you may feel awkward when you describe your new ideas. It is often difficult to see yourself in a different role. You will find yourself modifying or even changing, your original objective as you test yourself in the world.

2. You'll receive valuable feedback on how you come across. How are other people reacting to you? Are they confused by what you're saying? Are you unintentionally demeaning or disqualifying yourself? Find out what areas in your presentation you need to refine in order to make a good impression when it counts. Also, when the feedback is positive and encouraging, it will fill you with confidence and energy.

3. You'll get new ideas about how to realize your goals. When they hear your job description, your listeners may find they know people who do the work you're interested in. In this way, you'll learn job titles as well as names of organizations, fields, and industries that would fit your criteria.

4. You'll learn the names of people working in jobs similar to the one you describe. This information will lead to the second phase of networking, *informational interviewing.* Only by talking to people who are actually doing what you are considering can you (a) judge whether a certain field is right for you; (b) make important and valuable contacts; (c) uncover unadvertised job openings. Consider how much easier it will be to call a stranger when you can say, "Your cousin told me I should talk to you," than when you have no personal link at all.

PREPARATION

To get the most from your informal interviews, you'll need to take the following steps:

1. Have business cards printed. This is a must. Any print shop will make up simple cards showing your name, address, and telephone number. People save cards. That's how they will remember you. Scrawling your number on the bottom of your check stub or on a scrap of paper is not only inefficient, it looks tacky.

2. Have letterhead stationery printed with your name, address, and telephone number in a neat, businesslike typeface. (You will find a sample business card and letterhead at the end of this chapter.)

3. Dress appropriately. A major goal in these interviews, besides research, is to project a professional image that reflects the seriousness of your intentions. No matter whom you are meeting, wear businesslike clothes to set the tone. That doesn't necessarily mean wearing a "uniform" that someone else has prescribed. It does mean clean, neat clothes that have been chosen with careful attention to the kind of impression you want to make.

4. Don't assume anything. If you say to yourself, "There are no jobs out there like this," or "No one is going to hire me," you'll be creating self-fulfilling prophecies. False assumptions account for many missed opportunities. Wait until you have explored your idea thoroughly before coming to conclusions.

5. Remain focused. At the risk of belaboring this point, we stress again the fundamental importance of clarifying your goals. To attract help that is relevant and to avoid flying off in a thousand different directions, you must first know what you want. Your ability to describe it will help others see what you are after. If you completed the exercises in Chapter 2, you should be able to explain what you are looking for in less than thirty seconds.

6. You may not want your current employer to know that you are looking for a new job. In this case, you can discreetly engage in informal interviewing as long as you remember to ask your contacts to keep all discussions confidential.

THE PROCEDURE

Very briefly, informal interviewing includes the following steps:

1. Make a list of people you know personally with whom you feel comfortable.
2. Meet with them to discuss your career plans.
3. Ask them for ideas, resources, leads, and feedback.
4. Keep written records of all suggestions and your follow-up.
5. Follow up all informal interviews with thank-you letters.

1. Make a list of everyone you know.

When we ask our clients to write down the names of everyone they know, they look at us in disbelief. "Everyone?" they exclaim, discouraged by the enormity of the task. Let us assure you—the job isn't as tedious or as unwieldy as it might seem at first. When you start writing, the list grows quickly.

Begin with friends, family, neighbors, school chums, army buddies, and people you do business with, such as your accountant, stockbroker, hairdresser, dentist, and so on. Include only those people with whom you feel comfortable. Also write down the names of people in sales or service jobs whom you know casually. They are sure to have a lot of contacts and community awareness. For example, one woman, while having her dress altered, described to the tailor her dreams of being in the travel business. As it happened, the tailor's next client owned a travel agency and came in bemoaning the loss of an employee during a particularly busy period. The tailor gave the travel agent his previous client's card and a successful match was made.

Don't rule out acquaintances in other cities either. Another job hunter who had recently moved to our area wrote to friends back home and got wonderful suggestions, encouragement, and even the names of people to contact in the new city. As an added advantage, the letter writing gave him an opportunity to refine his objective.

Keep prodding yourself to make your list extensive. Really stretch your memory. You may not need to contact more than a few individuals on your list, but the last names may prove to be the most helpful. With such a list in hand, you never have to feel stuck. At any point in your job search, you will always have these names to come back to.

Consider Jon, who became very discouraged when, after three months of exploring computer sales, he realized it was not the field for him. Going back to his informal interview list, he recontacted friends to get some new ideas. This helped him get through a distressing time and quickly figure out a new direction.

2. Arrange appointments.

Look at your list and study your calendar. How many people could you see this week? Two? Three? Four? Check those individuals you would be willing to call to discuss your job hunt. Did you check your father? Uncle Fred? Will you tell your dentist during tomorrow's appointment? Don't disqualify anyone as a possible source of help. Studies reveal that the average adult knows 250 people. Thus, every contact you make potentially exposes you to another 250 possibilities. Exciting leads come from unexpected sources.

It is very important to set up face-to-face meetings, not just telephone conversations. Personal contact is infinitely more productive. To arrange these meetings, you might say something like "Aunt Sara, I am thinking about changing jobs. I'm not quite sure what I want to do, but I have been playing around with some ideas and I'd love to hear your advice. Could we meet whenever it's convenient for you . . . perhaps for lunch this week?"

3. Meet your contacts.

At the meetings, briefly describe your objective. Pay attention to your contacts' reactions. Do their eyes glaze over halfway through your first sentence? Learn where and when you need to polish your presentation. Every time you repeat your ideas you will find yourself becoming more confident and clear. Remember, these first attempts to describe new goals may feel clumsy, even embarrassing. That's why it's better to practice and experiment with a trusted friend than with a potential employer. Also, always ask, "Do you know anyone who may be doing what I am describing?" or "Can you think of someone I should talk to?"

4. Keep records.

Write down the names, addresses, and telephone numbers of any referrals; note the person who gave them to you. After many such discussions, you may forget who referred you to whom. Also, jot down any ideas and suggestions (see the sample form at the end of this chapter).

5. Send thank-you notes.

That's right—even send a note to Aunt Sara. A short, handwritten note of appreciation is all that's necessary. It is a nice gesture. It is also an important habit to start developing to maintain business contacts.

IN CONCLUSION

Once you start these informal conversations, your job search is well under way. You should find your network growing quickly. And since you've been dealing strictly with people you know, the process shouldn't hurt a bit. Far from writhing with the old job-search anxiety, you may even have enjoyed yourself by enriching old relationships and doing a bit of socializing. Your contacts, meanwhile, undoubtedly feel flattered at being sought out for advice.

Still, it's inevitable that you will experience some seemingly wasted encounters. But for every two, three, or four pointless discussions, you'll have had one that yields an enormous payoff. The more people you talk to, the greater will be your chances of success.

ONE FINAL NOTE

It's also a good idea to read about different occupations that interest you. Visit a public library or college career center. The federal government has some excellent material available through the Superintendent of Documents (U.S. Government Printing Office, Washington, D.C. 20402) or the federal bookstores. Ask them to send you some literature. In particular, the *Dictionary of Occupational Titles* and the *Occupational Outlook Handbook* are excellent general references for specific fields and are available in most libraries. These and other good sources of information are included in the Suggested Reading list at the back of this book.

Keep your ears and eyes open. Be a sponge, soaking up new information and ideas so you will be ready for the next step—informational interviewing.

INITIAL CONTACT LIST

Use this form to brainstorm a list of people who could be a part of your initial network.

WHO: Anyone you know: family, friends, neighbors, former business associates, teachers;
Anyone who provides a service and deals with the public: bankers, lawyers, politicians, clergy, civic leaders;
Anyone who earns a living by making contacts: salespeople, stockbrokers, real estate agents, insurance brokers.

WHY: To get names of people doing what you are interested in doing;
To get their initial reaction to your career goals and your presentation;
To get practice in interviewing and asking questions;
To get ideas.

HOW: Set up an appointment, state what you are considering, and ask for names, ideas, and suggestions.

NAME	ADDRESS	PHONE

MARKETING YOURSELF IN PRINT

Effective colors for stationery and business cards are gray and ivory. Consult with a typesetter or printer as to style of type, paper quality, and color. This is an important investment for job hunters, as it reflects your professionalism and personal style.

EXAMPLE OF BUSINESS STATIONERY

Jean Smithson
11200 Alahambra Drive
Washington, D.C. 20011

Jean Smithson
11200 Alahambra Drive
Washington, D.C. 20011

EXAMPLE OF BUSINESS CARDS

Jean Smithson
11200 Alahambra Drive
Washington, D.C. 20011
(202) 361-7198

ORGANIZING THE RESEARCH

RECORD KEEPING: After each interview for information and feedback, complete a record like this one.

CONTACT FILE: 5 × 7 cards or pages in a notebook.

Name: _____

Position: _____

Company/organization: _____

Address: _____

Phone: _____

Referral source: _____

Type of communication (letter, phone, interview):
_____

   Date: _____ Content: _____
_____

Referrals, suggestions: _____
_____

Follow-up strategy: _____
_____

Resume sent: _____ Date: _____

Thank-you sent: _____ Date: _____

4
INFORMATIONAL INTERVIEWING

Becoming happily employed involves more than just knocking on doors in search of an empty slot.

Finding the right job is a process of discovery and experimentation. It involves learning continually about yourself and the world, and clarifying, modifying, and refining your goals until you have hit upon a compatible and available niche. The key to expediting this process is networking. Informal interviewing, discussed in the preceding chapter, should have helped you come up with several job titles you would like to explore. Now we will take you one step further—researching those job titles.

The best way to learn more about particular jobs— and also to gain a competitive edge—is through *informational interviewing*, the second phase of networking. Simply put, informational interviewing means talking to people in jobs or fields that interest you, asking them questions about what they do and about their trade or profession. It's just what the term implies—you interview them for information.

THE OUTCOME

What's the purpose of informational interviewing? These interviews give you an ingenious, stress-free opportunity to talk to people in your areas of interest, learn about different companies, and, in some instances, present yourself to a potential employer without either of you feeling any pressure to make a decision. Richard Bolles, in his book *What Color Is Your Parachute?* says of this technique, "Any way you can let an executive window-shop you, without putting them on the spot, will create a very favorable situation for you." Likewise, you will be able to window-shop for the most appropriate working situation for yourself.

By interviewing people in the field, you can reap the following benefits:

1. You can find out before you make a commitment whether the job fits your criteria.

2. You can get your foot in the door. People will be more apt to meet you when you request an informational interview instead of a job interview. Even more appealing to them will be your interest in what are likely to be their favorite subjects—themselves and their work.

3. You will be enlarging your network by making contacts with people in the field. Remember, the name of the game is who you know and who knows you.

4. Your efforts and thoroughness in job hunting are likely to impress your contact, who may one day be in a position to hire you and is now in a position to help you.

5. You'll be bypassing the personnel office, which as a rule has no hiring power but exists only to screen applicants. Why risk disqualification before you can get to the person with authority?

6. You're relying on your own resources to find a position. You cannot rely exclusively on intermediaries like employment agencies or headhunters. They may be helpful, but beware of putting all your eggs in their basket.

7. You'll have an opportunity to learn the problems and needs of the industry/company/department as well as its jargon. This will work to your advantage in the hiring interview.

8. You'll find out about unadvertised openings or get ideas as to where new positions might be created.

9. If you want to work as an independent contractor, you can talk to those who have followed a similar career path or who have worked as free-lancers. They can motivate you and help you develop a successful strategy.

There is only one catch, and it is an important one. If you're going to do this right (and why do it if you're not?), you must follow the first commandment of informational interviewing: *Thou shalt not ask for a job. Thou shalt only seek information.*

Violating this rule will damage your efforts as well as your credibility. In short, break this rule and you could blow everything. At this point in your job search, you are not seeking to be hired but to learn more about a certain area in order to make a decision. True, a job might well result from your contact with people who have the power to hire, but, at this point, you are not yet ready to make a decision and seek a hiring interview.

It is important that this distinction be clear in your mind. If you are confused about the purpose of your visit, your interviewee will be confused too. You will wind up making a very poor impression. And if, deep in your heart, you don't give a hoot for the research and are really after a job offer, for heaven's sake, say so. Pretending otherwise could seem like deceit.

Informational interviews are a valuable means of learning and making contacts. Should you decide to apply for a job, you will have an advantage over an unfamiliar applicant. If, however, in the course of conversation, you are offered a job—which often occurs— it is advisable not to accept on the spot. For your own benefit, take some time to think it over.

THE PROCEDURE

Informational interviewing consists of four steps:
1. Arrange a face-to-face meeting, either by phone or by letter.

2. Meet with the interviewee to ask questions and obtain information.
3. Follow up with a thank-you note.
4. Maintain careful records of all communication and follow-up. (Use the contact file cards suggested on page 46).

More specifically, we suggest the following:

1. Contact people who are in jobs or organizations that are of interest of you.

Where do you find these people? (1) The list you compiled during your informal interviews (when Uncle Fred said, "You gotta talk to my bridge partner. . . . He's got a job exactly like the one you're describing"). (2) People you already know. (3) People you have read about or who are in companies you have seen advertised. (One of our most enterprising clients, who decided to go into advertising, called the head of almost every firm listed in the telephone book, getting appointments, leads, and subsequent offers.)

Many experts advise that you first write a letter to introduce yourself and explain your purpose, and then follow up with a phone call at a time stated in your letter (see page 59 for a sample letter). This approach is businesslike and time-saving in that it bypasses lengthy, sometimes awkward explanations over the phone. Writing a letter to someone you have read about in the newspaper may be very flattering to the recipient. However, you may feel it is more appropriate and comfortable to call directly. A good idea is to experiment with both.

2. Arrange appointments by telephone.

State your name and who referred you. ("I am Julie Jobhunter. Dr. Smith suggested I get in touch with you," or "I read the article about your firm in the *Tribune*.")

Explain the purpose of your call. ("I am exploring a career change and am very interested in marine biology, but I need to learn more about the field.")

Make it clear that you are not looking for a job, only

doing research. ("I am not asking for a job; I am not at that point yet. I would like to hear about what you do so I can learn about different opportunities.") You may need to elaborate since many people won't understand and will think you're asking for a job anyway! Still, keep the explanation brief and to the point.

Request a small block of time at their convenience. ("I would appreciate a chance to meet with you personally for about fifteen minutes, whenever it's convenient for you.")

3. Make every effort to schedule personal meetings.

Most people will be willing to see you. We suggest that you begin with people in fields that are not your first choice so you can gain some interview experience with those who are not crucial to you. Save the top companies and their executives until you have a clearer picture of the industry and can ask intelligent, sharply focused questions.

If someone refuses to meet with you, accept it gracefully and ask for a referral. ("I understand how busy you are, Mr. Rush; however, do you think you could recommend another person who might be able to help me?")

4. Write down the agreed-upon time and place and then reconfirm it.

You want to make darned sure you are there when you're supposed to be.

5. Prepare your questions ahead of time.

We suggest using the following questions as guidelines (you might write them on an index card and take it to the interview):

- Tell me about what you do. (A good opener. This will allow you to determine if the job requirements match your checklist of criteria.)
- What do you like about your job? What don't you like? (The latter helps you uncover the problems and needs you would face in a similar position. Also, you

will want to address these in a hiring interview. People are usually eager to voice their complaints to a willing listener.)
- What skills, experience, and training are necessary to enter this field? (As with all questions, don't draw any conclusions based on only one person's opinion. You need several points of view.)
- What is the earning potential? What salary range can I expect at my level? (This is important information to have in salary negotiations.)
- How did you become interested in this field? (People love to tell their life histories. This is a good way to learn about their goals and advancement strategies.)
- Who else should I talk to? (Never leave without asking this question. If they can't think of anyone, offer to call back in a few days.) Also: Are there any professional groups or publications I should know about?

6. Take time to develop rapport.

Even though you're prepared with questions, don't interrogate. Relax, make small talk, be casual, and let the conversation flow. Ask questions to keep the long-winded types from meandering off into irrelevant storytelling. But above all, use the time to create positive relationships while gathering useful information.

7. Leave at the agreed-upon time.

Don't be surprised if you are invited to stay longer, and feel free to do so, but make sure you acknowledge when your time is up.

8. Let your interviewee know that the meeting was helpful.

When you wrap up the conversation, express your appreciation. Letting people know they helped (come on, certainly you can find *something* that was of value!) makes them feel important. And any time you make people feel better about themselves, they will feel better about you. ("Thank you so much for taking this time, Mr. Rush. Your suggestion to get into sales for a year is excellent. I am going to call those two sales managers this afternoon. I'll let you know what happens.") When interviewees don't feel like they have helped, they'll have a bad feeling about themselves which they'll associate with you.

9. Leave a business card.

If they ask for your resume, you may want to send them one. Don't take your resume to an informational interview; this could be construed as: "I have a hidden agenda." Also, sending it later puts you back in their thoughts.

10. Write a thank-you note.

Mention again your appreciation, how you benefited, and what steps you have taken. Volunteer to keep them posted when their leads or suggestions prove fruitful.

11. Maintain an organized file system of all your meetings.

Record the dates, addresses, and phone numbers of your contacts. Write summaries of the interviews and the items discussed, including personal conversation. Mr. Rush will be terribly impressed when next you meet if you ask about his son's soccer team or how his bridge lessons have improved his game. Use your contact file cards for this. Also, keep track of your activity on the Statistics Sheet on page 55. Keeping records helps you evaluate your strategy.

12. Keep receipts for the expenses incurred in your job hunt.

If you are seeking employment in the same trade or business you're now in and you itemize deductions on Form 1040 (long form), you may declare job-hunting expenses as a tax deduction, even if you end up not changing jobs. Consult your accountant about this.

By interviewing for information, you are meeting and developing rapport with potential employers, discovering hidden job opportunities, and learning about the industry. When you write thank-yous on your letterhead and leave your business card, you are firmly planting your name in your contact's mind. Even if nothing happens with a particular company, there is always the chance your contacts will remember you and act as your advocate.

Take Betsy. She was interested in marketing for banks and made appointments to see the presidents of several major banks in the city. One chief executive, impressed with Betsy's assertiveness, happened to be at a party with a financial services VP who mentioned she needed a marketing director. The banker, remembering Betsy's card, suggested her for the job and she got it. Moral of the story: networking can work for you even when you're not around . . . and in surprising ways.

IN CONCLUSION

Informational interviewing is a low-stress, enjoyable means of developing valuable contacts and preparing yourself for getting hired. Nevertheless, it requires considerable *patience* (when those phone calls go unanswered and appointments keep getting changed), *stamina* (when you've scheduled meetings every day and must remain alert and enthusiastic), and *effort* (making yourself dial that phone one more time, mustering up the courage to call the company president).

Often, you'll feel like you are getting nowhere. That seems to be an inevitable part of the process. Don't get discouraged. If you are clear about the kind of work you want and understand how to investigate possible options, if you are receptive and flexible while remaining focused and directed, and if you're willing to throw yourself wholeheartedly into the search with dogged determination, willing to take the necessary risks and plow on even when you don't feel like it—you'll find the job you've targeted for yourself and learn a great deal in the process.

STATISTICS SHEET

This sheet gives you a picture of what you do every week. Remember we told you that job hunting is a numbers game. By keeping track of your numbers, you can see what you are doing with your time. You can evaluate what is working and what isn't. You can decide what you need to do more of and where you might want to cut back.

Week of: _____

1. Number of phone contacts: _____
   Informational interviews set: _____
   Referrals: _____
   Hiring interviews set: _____

2. Letters sent: Response to an ad: _____
                  Referral introduction: _____
                  Cold introduction: _____
                  Thank-you: _____
                  Follow-up: _____

3. Interviews conducted:
   Informal: _____ Informational: _____ Hiring:_____

4. Other: _____
   _____
   _____

Summary (what I learned this week): _____
   _____
   _____
   _____

Plans next week: _____
   _____
   _____
   _____

RESEARCH PLANNING CHART

As you begin to identify areas of career interest and specific industries, you will want a simple tool for keeping track in an organized way of potential employers and key contacts within the organization.

This chart is one method of organizing this sometimes overwhelming phase of job research. Make a separate chart for each area you are exploring and add information as you research and interview for information.

Area of Interest, Position _____

POTENTIAL EMPLOYERS	CONTACTS IN COMPANY/ POSITION	ADDRESS/ PHONE	REFERRAL SOURCE

RESEARCHING
THE JOB MARKET

Use this worksheet as a guideline for formulating interview questions and recording information about each job you investigate. You'll notice that it will also prepare you for the hiring interview.

JOB TITLE: _____

1. Nature of Work, Job Responsibilities: _____

   _____

   _____

   _____

2. Working Conditions: _____

   _____

   _____

   _____

3. Places of Employment: _____

   _____

   _____

   _____

4. Training, Other Qualifications, and Advancement:

   _____

   _____

   _____

   _____

5. Employment Outlook (Job Security, Availability):

   _____

   _____

   _____

6. Earnings: _____

7. What interests of mine will be satisfied in this job?

_____

_____

_____

_____

8. What personality traits do I have that match those needed for success in this job? _____

_____

_____

_____

9. Which of my needs and values can be met in this job? _____

_____

_____

_____

10. Which skills and special knowledge do I have that are needed for this job? _____

_____

_____

_____

11. Which new skills and special knowledge will I need to develop for this type of job? _____

_____

_____

_____

SAMPLE LETTER REQUESTING AN INFORMATIONAL INTERVIEW

Harold Snow
3853 Colson Avenue
San Francisco, California   94105

January 3, 1984

Correct name and title

Mr. J. B. Connors
Director of Communications
First Union Bank
600 Market Street
San Francisco, California   94132

Appropriate salutation

Dear Mr. Connors,

State your purpose in writing

Jim O'Brien suggested that I contact you to learn more about the communications field.

Who are you?

For five years, I have been employed in personnel management and am ready to make a career switch.

Why he should meet with you

I'm just in the process of exploring and not ready to make a commitment, but I would love to learn more about your field. I would appreciate fifteen minutes of your time at your convenience to ask your advice and get some suggestions.

Ask for follow-up

I will phone you on Wednesday to see if we can arrange a meeting.

Polite closing

Sincerely,

Signature

Harold Snow

5
THE
RESUME

It's a basic fact of job hunting:
you are going to need a resume.

The best time to start putting a resume together is
now, after you have come up with a job description.

THE PURPOSE

Why is a resume so important? First of all, you don't
want to be caught without one when you are asked for
it. And it is likely you will be asked often, whether it
be by your next-door neighbor, the president of Widg-
ets, Inc., or in response to a want ad. A resume is an
important part of the networking process. People will
want your resume for all sorts of reasons: "In case something comes up, let me keep it on file," or "If I hear of
something, I'll pass it along," or "Send me your resume,
and we'll take a look at it." Resumes are introductions
to get you in the door for job interviews. They are also
memory joggers to be sent to people after informational
interviews.

We encourage you to write the resume yourself. The
very process of putting together this document helps
you organize your thoughts for the hiring interview.
Having to think through your skills, experiences, and
objective enables you to be more articulate in the job
interview. It may be laborious, but it will help you in
the long run.

THE PROCEDURE

We know that the task of writing a resume can be tedious and time consuming. We strongly urge you not to do it all in one sitting. Instead, set up a schedule:

1. Begin by listing on paper all your past jobs, paid or volunteer. Write down everything you did, accomplished, and enjoyed in each one. (See Resume Inventory Sheets on page 66.)
2. Take a break for at least a few hours.
3. Scan resume-writing books, learning from examples.
4. Spend one to two hours organizing the information you wrote out in step 1.
5. Take a break
6. Refine, modify, edit, organize.
7. Take a break. The rhythm of backing away, then rewriting keeps you fresh, alert, and creative.
8. Again, refine and edit.
9. Ask friends to critique your draft.

THE FORMAT

Information should be organized under broad headings, depending on which of the following formats you choose. You have a choice of three basic plans and alternatives, but you can also devise variations. Sample formats are included at the end of this chapter.

Chronological Format

The chronological resume is a listing of your work experience and educational history in chronological order. The broad headings are typically job objective, work experience, education and perhaps honor achievements, and memberships. All categories highlight previous job experience and education with brief descriptions that relate to your job objective. This format is most commonly used when changing jobs in the same field, in which case continuous work activity needs to be documented.

Functional Format

The functional resume organizes your experience according to skills or functions. The broad headings are skill categories and the information under each skill demonstrates your capabilities through a variety of work, volunteer, and personal experiences. This format is best for a career changer, a volunteer, or a person who wants to reenter the work force after an absence or who has had an uneven employment record.

Combination Format

In this resume, headings are a combination of skills and work history. This format gives both the job changer and career changer an excellent opportunity to present capabilities and transferable skills combined with a record of work experience. We generally encourage this type of resume.

ALTERNATIVES TO THE RESUME

The Qualifications Brief and Biographical Sketch

These can be used by people who are self-employed and need to market their own professional expertise. For example, a management consultant who wants to market her speaking, facilitation, and problem-solving skills would use this form as an information sheet describing her education and qualifications. There would be specific mention of former clients, types of presentations, and services she offers. These may be written in paragraph form rather than the one-line descriptions used in resumes.

The Career Portfolio

A portfolio is a cumulative display of what you produced as a volunteer, student, or professional. It includes examples of creative work (paintings, writing samples, designs, or layouts) that relate to the position for which you are applying. Includes only a few examples of your best work. An overflowing portfolio overwhelms, detracts from your presentation, and diminishes the impact of your work. For a volunteer, a portfolio helps demonstrate the valuable skills you gained in unpaid work. It might include recommendations, examples of public recognition, and samples of written work.

WRITING THE COVER LETTER

A resume without a cover letter is like an unannounced salesperson showing up at your door. If you are going to let a perfect stranger in, you at least want to see credentials. This is exactly what a cover letter does— it introduces you, a total stranger, to the reader. The letter must be compelling, personable, and brief. It should relate specifically to the position in question. Keep in mind you have only eight seconds to convince the reader to invite you in.

The cover letter should include three parts:

The Opening

Begin with a statement about your purpose in sending your resume. Why are you writing? What do you want from the reader? Are you responding to a want ad or the advice of a friend? An example of an opening is, "Jane Smith, the editor of *Consumer Affairs*, suggested I contact you about a position as managing editor of your journal."

The Main Body

In two or three sentences, describe who you are and how your unique strengths and abilities could benefit the employer. Emphasize and support these skills. Your research of the company can be helpful here in addressing its specific needs. For example: "As editor of *Community Health Care* magazine, I have been able to translate medical terminology into clear, readable text. My ability to do this has had a direct impact on the increased number of requests for health services."

The Closing

Express your willingness to provide more information by letter or in person. State a specific time you intend to get in touch or something more general like "I'll be available to meet with you at your earliest convenience."

DO'S AND DON'TS OF RESUMES AND COVER LETTERS

Consider this: ninety-eight out of one hundred unsolicited resumes get tossed in the trash every day. We want to help you write a resume and cover letter that not only gets read but leads to an interview. Review the sample resumes in this chapter as well as in books listed in the Bibliography, and study the following tips.

DO:

1. Use plain English, not jargon.
2. State your job objective at the top. Don't make the reader have to work to figure out your career goals. (Use the Job Description exercises on pages 31–34 for writing up an objective.)
3. Make your resume no more than two pages. Every statement on it should relate to the job objective.
4. Watch your spelling and punctuation. Avoid typographical errors. (First impressions are the deciding factor.)
5. Use factual, concise language. Describe your accomplishments with action verbs and hard-hitting adjectives.
6. Emphasize your positive skills and abilities but be truthful. Some of the information may be investigated.
7. Print your resume on good-quality white or ivory bonded paper. Either typeset it or use a laser printer.
8. Have at least three knowledgeable people critique your resume before you draft your final copy.
9. Keep old resumes for future use.

10. Send a cover letter with each resume. Type the letter on your business stationery.
11. Use specific numbers and figures to demonstrate results. Not "I managed a staff," but "I managed a staff of fifteen." Not "successfully marketed new products," but "increased sales of new products 31 percent by developing a creative marketing strategy."

DON'T:

1. Send carbon copies.
2. Include salary information. (It's negotiable, so why limit yourself?)
3. List references on your resume. Instead, prepare a typed list of references, including name, position, address, and phone. Take this with you to the interview.
4. Address a cover letter "To Whom It May Concern." Always have a specific name.
5. Include personal data, such as weight, age, and marital status. You never know when this can work against you.

Worksheets and examples follow this section to help you organize and write your resume.

Exercise 1
RESUME INVENTORY SHEETS

Fill out a sheet for every job you have ever had, including volunteer positions, over the past ten years. It may help to go back to the skill lists in Chapter 2 to give you a vocabulary of skills. This becomes the data bank for your resume.

JOB TITLE: _____
(e.g., Personnel Specialist)

ORGANIZATION: _____ **DATES:** _____
(e.g., Community Hospital)　　　　　(e.g., 1982 to 1986)

What Did You Do? Specific Activities	What Skills and Special Knowledge Did You Use?	What Was a Positive Result?

Exercise 2
WRITING SKILL PHRASES

The purpose of this exercise is to help you write statements that demonstrate your skills:

1. Review your skill-clustering chart from page 25.
2. Add any new skills from your Resume Inventory Sheets.
3. Choose the top two to three skill clusters that include the majority of your skills.
4. Write a short descriptive phrase explaining how you can use each skill. Use adjectives, action verbs, and nouns to illustrate each skill specifically.
5. Rewrite and rewrite. Do not try to make your first attempts perfect.

EXAMPLE:

Skill Cluster No. 1 ADMINISTRATION
Direct a staff to achieve organizational objectives
Develop and administer departmental budget
Serve on administrative team as advisor
Interview, hire, and terminate employees
Present program proposal to management

Skill Cluster No. 2 PROMOTIONAL

Communicate concepts, policies, and procedures to all levels of management and staff
Promote organizational image and programs to community
Build and maintain contacts
Conduct market research studies and recommend alternatives
Design marketing strategies for implementing new services in the community and business

Skill Cluster No. 3 PLANNING AND ORGANIZATION
Plan and coordinate complex activities for multi-unit organization
Develop effective management and delivery systems
Develop hiring policies
Design and implement training programs

Exercise 3
ORGANIZING THE RESUME DATA

Begin writing a rough draft that compiles the information gathered in the previous two exercises.

It is helpful to think of the resume as being organized into three parts:

I. PERSONAL INFORMATION (name, address, telephone numbers)

II. JOB OBJECTIVE (kind of position, using these skills, in this kind of organization, solving these problems)

III. PAST EXPERIENCE (skill offerings, work experience, education, honors, achievements)

In the illustration below, the left-hand column contains descriptions of each resume category. On the right are specific examples this person chose to use.

James Potts
3800 West Armourdale
Carrollton, Texas 75007
(214) 323-5896

Job objective describing the kind of job you are seeking	**Job Objective:** Management position which integrates my administrative, planning, and organizational skills
1. Major skill cluster with skill phrases describing each sub-skill or one list of skills. **2. Prioritize all skills.** **3. Use present tense of action verbs.**	**Capabilities:** Administration • Direct a staff to achieve objectives • Communicate policies and procedures to staff Planning and organization • Develop effective management system • Plan and coordinate complex activities for a multi-unit organization

OR

Capabilities:
- Plan and coordinate complex activities for a multi-unit organization
- Develop effective management system
- Direct a staff to achieve objectives
- Communicate policies and procedures

Date of employment (most recent first), position, company/organization, and location

Work Experience:
1979—Present
Director of Personnel,
Community Hospital,
Dallas, Texas

Brief description of duties

Managed more than five hundred employees, professional and hourly
Responsible for all human resource functions

Cite accomplishments that support capabilities (past tense of action verbs)

- Served as member of policy-making administrative staff of a $45 million business
- Designed and implemented first employee-training program

Degree, institution, date, honors, activities

Education:
M.B.A., Management,
University of Colorado, 1980
B.A., Personnel Administration,
University of Colorado, 1976

Affiliations, honors, professional responsibilities and activities that capabilities support

Professional:
Personnel Management Association: Chairman of Community Relations, responsible for promoting the professional image of the organization and the credibility of its members to the business community
Chamber of Commerce: Finance Committee, worked with small businesses to create more economic activity and development of long-range plans

Community activities

Community:
United Way Chairperson, supervisor of thirty-person fund-raising team

Language fluency, military experience, extensive travel, and anything that is pertinent to job objective

Personal:
Have lived in the Dallas area for twenty years

Type references on separate sheet of stationery to bring to interview

References:
Available upon request

Chronological

Recent college graduate. Emphasize education and extracurricular activities.

Steven James
127 St. Paul Street
Brookline, Massachusetts 02146
(617)273-2292

Job Objective: Seeking a position with advancement opportunity that combines a mathematics background with business administration

Education: Boston University, Boston, Massachusetts

B.A., Mathematics, 1981

Special emphasis in business administration, including computer programming, accounting, economics, and management

Extracurricular Activities: Treasurer of national social fraternity—responsible for all financial transactions and obligations and for collecting payments from members and maintaining files and records

Vice president of senior class—responsible for public relations within the university and with the community

Experience:

Summers 1979 & 1980 Filene's, Boston, Massachusetts
Sales clerk in men's and boys' department
• Increased experience and responsibility with sales, customer relations, and inventory work
• Asked to work in other departments because of adaptability and communications skills

Summer 1978 Filene's, Credit Department, Boston, Massachusetts
• Received and filed payments
• Researched applications for credit
• Established consumer relations with customers

Summer 1976 McDonald's, Framingham, Massachusetts
• Cashiered and did bookkeeping for the manager

References: Available upon request

Chronological

Chronological Format for Changing Jobs in the Same Field. Continuous work experience is best documentation for changing jobs within the same field.

Louse Brockman
1125 Green Street
San Francisco, California 94109
(415) 435-0110

Objective:
A position in development and fund-raising with an innovative organization allowing me to utilize my executive skills and experience

Work Experience and Accomplishments:

1978–Present Executive Director, Baldwin College Alumni Association, Santa Clara, California
Responsible for all phases of the association's $950,000 operation, long-range planning, external relations, program design, and leadership to a staff of twenty people
- Developed a strategic long-range plan that prioritized goals, including the implementation of twelve new programs. Directed a marketing program that increased membership by 20 percent and income by 11 percent during the past three years (1985–88)
- Developed a sophisticated computer-records data base system to record annual gifts of approximately $10 million and retrieve information for all university users
- Increased annual operating revenues from $284,000 to more than $1 million

1969–1978 Associate Director, Vice President, Baldwin College Endowment Association
Responsible for all fund-raising, direct-mail, and telefund solicitations, volunteer recruitment and training, and special campaigns; and served as the top assistant to the chief executive officer
- Recruited and trained more than one thousand volunteers and directed more than seventy telefund campaigns
- Initiated a $100 undesignated gift club, which now generates $50,000 per year for the foundation
- Administered total gifts of $15.7 million from 88,000 donors and cultivated major-donor million-dollar prospects

Community Activities:
United Way, Chairperson, supervised team of fifty fundraisers
Rotary Club, Board Member and Youth Affairs Chairperson

Education:
1969   M.A. in Education, Baldwin College, Santa Clara, California
1968   B.S. in Business Administration, Baldwin College

References: Furnished upon request

Functional

Reentry with emphasis on volunteer work experience. Functional Format for de-emphasizing lack of work experience.

Glen Harrison
125 Euclid
Tempe, Arizona 85281
(602) 991-4685

Job Objective:
A position which integrates skills and experience in creative planning, coordination, and promotion of projects and events

Strengths:
- role model and effective team builder
- conscientious and dependable person
- confident communicator and manager
- creative problem solver
- high-energy person
- innovative project developer and coordinator
- facilitator and trainer
- promoter of products and services

Experience:

1981–Present American Diabetes Association, Phoenix, Arizona
Coordinator of Annual Fund-raising Campaign
Responsible for planning, coordinating, and managing annual campaign
- Raised an average of $250,000 annually
- Developed concept of telethon, which involves over five hundred volunteers
- Solicited major corporate donors
- Served as association liaison to the media

1980–1985 Voluntary Action Center, Phoenix, Arizona
Chairman of Public Relations
Created innovative programs for promoting community programs, which doubled the number of people utilizing center's referral services

1975–1979 Goldwaters Department Store, Phoenix, Arizona
Sales Clerk, Fashion Accessories

Education:
1971 University of Southern California B.A., Sociology

References: Available upon request

Combination
Functional/Chronological
Emphasize skills and work accomplishments.

Robert Donovan
3642 Westview Drive
Atlanta, Georgia 30314
(404) 572-2181

Objective:
Management position allowing me to utilize my planning, organizing, and administrative skills

Executive Skills Summary:
- Strategic Planning
- Project Management
- Research and Analysis
- Administration
- Personnel Management
- Communication
- Technical Competence

Work Experience and Accomplishments:
Director of Personnel Community Hospital, Savannah, Georgia, March 1979—present
Responsible for all aspects of the human resource management function for five hundred plus professional and hourly employees providing health care services
- Served as a member of the policy-making administrative staff of a $45 million business
- Researched and wrote new employee handbook and coordinated a committee in the preparation of a supervisory manual
- Updated comprehensive benefits program resulting in cost savings and improved services to employees
- Advised management personnel in all areas of manpower planning and utilization

Director of Support Services, Community Hospital, March 1978—March 1979
Responsible for staffing, budgeting, and development of policies and procedures for a multi-unit division providing clinical and support services
- Developed and administered $6 million budget for a multi-unit division consisting of eight departments and 120 employees
- Conducted manpower utilization study with an outside consulting group which resulted in increased productivity and a $62,000 salary savings
- Supervised a staff of professionals providing key support services including materials management, record administration, and food service

Personnel Specialist, State of Georgia Office for Planning
and Programming, February 1976–March 1978
Provided consulting services to county and municipal
governments in establishing and/or refining personnel
management systems
Served as the personnel officer for this state agency
- Developed total personnel management systems for
  counties and cities which previously had no formalized
  systems
- Provided a variety of technical services to governmental
  units including designing salary systems and
  classification plans; also advised concerning FLSA,
  EEOC, collective bargaining, and preventive labor
  relations
- Presented program proposals to top governing boards in a
  manner that encouraged acceptance and implementation

Community Activities:
United Way Chairperson, supervised team of thirty fund-
raisers
Board of Deacons, Valley Presbyterian Church

Education:
1980, M.B.A., Management. Wharton School, University of
Pennsylvania
1976, B.A., Personnel Administration, Morehouse College

Resume Alternative: The Biographical Sketch

JANE M. MCGUIRE

As a career consultant, Jane McGuire is in the business of conserving human resources. She helps individuals find satisfying career directions and helps employers stimulate productivity using an innovative career planning process.

Ms. McGuire helps individuals identify their most valuable resources—their skills and abilities—and turn them into a set of criteria for selecting the right career, the right job, and in the employer's case, for increasing productivity.

In addition to counseling individual job hunters and career changers, Ms. McGuire has designed and conducted numerous seminars and workshops for such organizations as Women in Communication, area College Marketing Associations, Women in Radio-Television, Home Economists in Business, the Washington Press Club, and the American Management Association. She has also lectured at the University of Massachusetts, and has participated in career seminars sponsored by American University and George Washington University and the federal government.

Workshop and seminar topics for special interest groups and companies include:

- Skills Analysis
- Success Strategies
- Self-marketing Techniques
- Researching the Hidden Job Market
- Organizing the Job Search
- Goal Setting
- Resume Writing
- Interviewing Techniques
- Job Burnout/Job Enrichment
- Time/Stress Management
- Leadership Development
- Office Politics

Ms. McGuire has served as a resource for newspaper articles and has appeared on local television and radio programs.

A graduate of the University of Maryland, Ms. McGuire spent seven years as a secondary teacher in Baltimore, Maryland, holds an M.A. in Guidance and Counseling from the University of Maryland, and is a member of the American Personnel and Guidance Association, the National Vocational Guidance Association, and the American Society for Training and Development.

Cover Letter for a Resume

John Green
1201 West 31 Street
Washington, D.C. 20009
January 10, 1984

Ms. Alice Needle, President
Robot Technology, Inc.
217 West Seventh Street
Portland, Oregon 97203

Dear Ms. Needle,

Purpose in writing Recently I learned through Dr. Eugene Mott, a professor in computer science at the Community College of Washington, D.C., of the expansion of your company's sales operations to Maryland and Virginia. I would like to be considered for any newly created sales positions.

State qualifications I have a broad knowledge of computer technology, having completed course work in the field as well as having work experience in computer sales, promotion, and market research. As a sales representative with a computer hardware firm, I was responsible for a two-state region which brought in sales of $1 million in one year.

Request follow-up For your review, I am enclosing my resume. I would appreciate a personal interview with you to learn more about your company and to discuss my application. If you plan to be in Washington in the near future, please let me know and I can arrange to meet with you.

Sincerely,

John Green

enc.

Letter Answering a Blind Advertisement

Susan Schmidt
6801 Oak
Oakland, California 94607

Ms. Sara Abrams
P.O. Box 673
Palo Alto, California 94303

Dear Ms. Abrams,

Purpose in writing

In response to the advertisement in the *San Jose Mercury News*, December 27, I am making application for the position described as an experienced writer for an advertising department of an industrial corporation.

Address your qualifications to those given in ad

My qualifications, as detailed in my resume, match the described position. I have had an internship in industrial advertising and earned a B.A. in English with additional course work in the area of writing and communications skills. My writing experience has included writing and editing brochures, sales promotions, press releases, and magazine articles. My background familiarized me with the consumer population to which you are directed, and I feel greatly enhances my qualifications as a communicator.

Ask for follow-up

I am available for an interview and would like the opportunity to discuss this position and my qualifications in more detail.

Sincerely,

Susan Schmidt

enc. resume

Thank-You Letter Following an Interview

Deborah Mysak
135 East 67 Street
Chicago, Illinois 60637

January 1, 1984

Ms. Carla Overton
Apex Industries
614 South Michigan Avenue
Chicago, Illinois 60605

Dear Ms. Overton,

Expressing your positive impressions

I greatly enjoyed our discussion today regarding the position of new product manager at Apex Industries.

Restate qualifications

I was very impressed with the plant operation and the personnel. I strongly believe that my management experience and technical abilities qualify me for this position with Apex, and appreciate your consideration of me for this job.

Closing

Thank you for your time and interest. I look forward to hearing from you soon.

Sincerely,

Deborah Mysak

6
GETTING HIRED

An interview is to employment
what courtship is to marriage.

Eventually you will find that you have collected enough information in your job search to be sure of your direction. The change will come when someone expresses an interest in you, or you have pinpointed a place you'd like to work or a job you'd like to have. At this point, you will start setting up a new kind of appointment: the *hiring interview*.

MOVING TOWARD AN INTERVIEW

The traditional routes to getting a job interview include the following:

Responding to want ads. A good idea—sometimes. About 17 percent of the time, jobs result. Even when they don't, you will get a lot of interviewing practice.

Visiting employment agencies. They can be helpful. Find one that specializes in your field, industry, or function. How? Call the best companies in your industry and find out which recruiting firms they use. Ask colleagues and friends. Look in the phone book or in directories at the library. Most people don't realize that there are three different kinds of placement firms, divided according to salary levels.

Employment agencies generally place people in office support positions paying under $35,000. They find applicants primarily through want ads and walk-ins. Many are paid by the employer (1 percent of each $1,000 of the candidate's salary); some are paid by the applicants. Be sure to read the contract very carefully. Very often, agencies have a temporary placement service. Unemployed job seekers can find temporary work until a permanent position comes along.

Recruiting firms place people in technical, professional, or mid-management positions with salaries ranging from $30,000 to $75,000. Recruiters, or headhunters, search for candidates to fill specific positions. They collect their fees from the employer upon placement—usually 25 to 30 percent of the candidate's first year's salary.

Executive search firms run in-depth searches to find senior-level executives for positions paying over $75,000. These firms are usually paid whether they fill the opening or not. Their fees are at least a third of the candidate's first year's compensation package.

Call several firms to determine whether they can help you. On page 90 you will find questions to help you screen an agency. Executive recruiters are harder to get in to see than employment consultants. Though recruiters tend to seek out candidates who are already happily and successfully employed, they are worth contacting. Perhaps you can get a referral from your informational interviews. Call or send your resume. They will want to know your background, salary level, and geographical requirements. If you fit their qualifications, they will probably keep your resume on file.

- **Mailing out unsolicited resumes.** Exhausting and, by and large, unproductive. Companies respond to about 1 out of 245 resumes received.

- **Contacting the company's personnel department.** Not usually very fruitful. These departments exist mainly to screen out applicants.

In addition to these traditional ways of getting an interview, there is a more creative route:

- **Call your contacts in** the targeted companies where you had informational interviews. Tell them you have finished exploring possibilities and have made some decisions.
- **Let them know that you benefited from their help** and were impressed with their organization.
- **Tell them you would appreciate any leads** and/or would like the opportunity to talk about what you could do for them as an employee of their firm.
- **Contact people you haven't met but who have possible job openings** to discuss your career exploration and their organizations. This will get you in the door of a person with the power to hire and helps you to continue the research and decision-making process.
- **Become active in professional associations** in your field. Many have job hot lines and placement services. Each person you meet is a potential referral source.

Job hunting is a numbers game. Generally, the more people you see, the more likely your success. Use every method you can—traditional and creative—to set up interviews. Then, once in the door, it's up to you to convince the interviewer you are the best candidate for the job.

The next step is to make a winning impression.

THE PROCEDURE

Do beads of perspiration form on your forehead and trickle down your armpits at the mere mention of a job interview? Relax. There's no need to panic. We can show you how to control the interview and turn it into a positive experience. How?

Let's put this formidable event into perspective. Recognize that you are selling a product—yourself—and that you have very limited time—twenty-six minutes on average—in which to convince a potential employer that you are the best person for the job. There are four important steps to achieving this goal:

1. Prepare ahead of time.
2. Concentrate on building rapport.
3. Be specific in explaining how the company will benefit from hiring you.
4. Follow the prepared guidelines listed later in this chapter.

1. Prepare, prepare, prepare.

If you have followed the steps in the preceding chapters, you are well ahead of the game. You are clear about the position you are seeking, why you want it, and what personal qualities and skills enable you to perform it well. Interviewers have no patience for wishy-washy applicants with fuzzy goals and poor self-knowledge.

Once you have a target, familiarize yourself with the organization and the field. If your Informational Interviewing gave you only an overview, take steps to obtain more specific information.

- Ask a stockbroker for literature on the company.
- Ask the reference librarian at a local library for ideas and information.
- Talk to employees, past and present, and to employees of competitors.
- Take tours of the facilities and of the competition's.
- Pay attention to media ads and related articles.

In pursuing these sources, find out all you can about:

- The company's philosophy and policies;
- Its products and services;
- Its age, size, growth rate, and growth pattern;
- Its problems, challenges, and needs;
- Its future projections, goals, and values;
- The competitors of the department in which your job would be;
- The names of key individuals in the firm.

Gathering all this information for the interview will both bolster your self-confidence and impress the interviewer with your initiative.

Here's a useful tip: make an individual "prep sheet" for each interview (see the Employment Interview

Checklist on pages 90—91). Record every piece of information and every idea that could possibly be useful in the interview itself. This will help you organize and remember what you have learned.

2. Concentrate on building rapport.

An interview is to employment what courtship is to marriage: an opportunity to make an impression and create a relationship that will lead to something more permanent.

In trying to sell yourself and impress another, it is easy to forget that hiring decisions are usually arbitrary and subjective. *The Wall Street Journal* reported that more hiring decisions are based on personal chemistry than on any other factor, including skills.

How do you create the right chemistry? First, realize it won't always happen. Just as not every date ends with a marriage proposal, not every interview concludes with a new job offer (thank goodness for both!). Nevertheless, you can maximize your chances for success by using a little psychology.

All human behavior is motivated by needs and the drive to satisfy them. Therefore, your trump card lies in identifying the other person's needs and showing how you can satisfy them.

In the context of the hiring interview, the first need is personal and emotional. Your interviewer, being a mere mortal, needs to feel important and loved. You can fulfill this need in the interview. The key, above all else, is to concentrate on making the interviewer feel good about him or herself. When you express sincere admiration, warmth, and enthusiasm, people will feel as if you like them. Consequently, they will feel good about themselves, and likely respond favorably to you. They'll relax and enjoy the meeting. On the other hand, if you are cold, uptight, judgmental, or in any way threaten their self-esteem or cause them to doubt their effectiveness, their defenses will shoot up. The relationship crumbles and you've lost your chance.

The second factor has to do with the job. In your research, you should have discovered the specific needs of the company, department, position, and boss. Sell yourself by demonstrating how your skills and experience can satisfy those needs or solve their problems.

3. Sell benefits.

It is not enough to sell your skills. Don't simply tell them what you are capable of doing. You need to take it one step further. You need to spell out exactly how your boss and the organization will benefit from hiring you. How will your skills help them solve their problems, do their job better, save them time or money, or make a profit?

Remember, everyone operates out of self-interest ("What's in it for me?"). If you can show the interviewer not only what you offer but what advantages your talents will give him or her specifically, you're a step ahead of your competition.

4. Follow the guidelines.

Use the following guidelines as a checklist before, during, and after the hiring interview.

BEFORE THE INTERVIEW:

- When you set up the appointment, be sure to write down the name, address, and time, and then verify this information before hanging up.
- Show up a few minutes early.
- Dress conservatively, avoiding extremes. While your appearance won't get you the job, it can definitely disqualify you.

BRING THE FOLLOWING:

- A notepad and pencil in case you need to record information during the discussion or make notes afterward;
- At least two copies of your resume (even if the interviewer already has one on file);
- Your Social Security number;
- Names and addresses of at least three references typed on your stationery and any letters of recommendation you may have;
- A portfolio of your work with samples and any supportive materials (such as articles about yourself).

AT THE OPENING OF THE INTERVIEW:

- When introduced, make a conscious effort to remember names. (Better yet, try to learn them in advance.)
- Greet the interviewer, making sure to pronounce his or her name correctly.
- Let the interviewer take the lead in shaking hands, and sit when asked.
- Avoid smoking or chewing gum, even if invited to do so.
- Engage in a few minutes of small talk to break the ice and establish rapport. Look for common interests. ("I see by the picture on your desk that your son plays soccer. . . . So does mine.")
- Body language is a powerful tool: lean forward, make eye contact, and look interested, but don't exaggerate.
- Have an opening statement prepared. You may not use it, but you'll feel better having something to say.

IN GETTING DOWN TO THE BUSINESS OF THE INTERVIEW:

- Keep your responses to the point. The interviewer wants to find out as much relevant information as possible in a limited amount of time. In essence, he or she wants to know: (1) Are you competent? and (2) Will you and the firm be compatible?
- Think before you talk.
- Talk in specifics, not generalities. For example, rather than "I like to work with people," say, "My experience in the Peace Corps has taught me how to get along and motivate people under all kinds of conditions."
- Don't mumble or ramble on.
- Describe your accomplishments, not your duties. Rather than "I was supervisor," say, "I supervised thirteen people and had responsibility for a budget in excess of $750,000.'
- Be sensitive to the interviewer's body language. When people stop focusing their eyes on you, and start shuffling papers, they are sending you a message: "I'm losing interest," or "I don't follow." Respond to the silent message by altering your course. For example, say, "Perhaps I should say this in another way," or "Am I making myself clear?"

- Be prepared with the major points you want to make and possible answers to tricky questions. Ask yourself, "If I were in the interviewer's seat, what would I want to know?" Practice on a tape recorder or with a partner, making sure you create opportunities to inject these points.
- Highlight the parts of your experience and the skills that directly relate to the position.
- If the interviewer tests your mettle with intimidating or stressful techniques, keep cool, be diplomatic, and remain gracefully assertive. Don't lash back or attack.
- Welcome objections. Remember that as long as they are unspoken, they will be barriers to your getting ahead. Get them out in the open and overcome them. Then, if you want the job, pleasantly and firmly prove them to be unfounded.
- Always be honest. Even though you need not volunteer negative information, answer truthfully when questioned.

AT THE CLOSE OF THE INTERVIEW:
- Let the interviewer initiate the close.
- If you are offered a job, you need not respond on the spot. Take some time to think it over.
- No job offer? Don't be discouraged. This is normal for the first few interviews, since all candidates must be carefully considered. The purpose of the first, even second, interview is to get invited back for another. The interviewing process can be a long, drawn-out affair.
- Don't talk money until you are offered the job. You will be in a better negotiating position that way. Talk opportunity, not security, in the early stages.
- Make sure you leave on a positive note. Shake hands, indicate your interest, and ask when a decision will be made.

THE FOLLOW-UP:
- Evaluate your experience. Don't punish yourself unmercifully for anything less than perfection. Was the meeting friendly? Did you get your points across?
- A well-written follow-up note is appropriate. It should convey an image of confidence, competence, and

enthusiasm. Include or reiterate important points.
- A follow-up call is also prudent—if you're not a pest. Ask, during the interview, if you can check back after a certain period of time.
- If you don't get the job, learn from your experience. We encourage clients to recontact the interviewer and ask for feedback. It may feel awkward, but it can give you invaluable insight as well as job leads.
- Consider taking a less than ideal job as a way to get your foot in the door and use the position as a spring-board to your career goals.
- Don't get discouraged when interviews don't pan out. The path to becoming happily employed is paved by "no, no, no, no," but it eventually leads to a final "yes."

If you get the job, congratulations. However, we urge you not to jump at the first offer or take anything too quickly that doesn't mesh with your criteria. The point, remember, is to become *happily*, not just gainfully employed. Also, as is often the case if you wait, you may have several offers to choose from.

How do you decide which job to take? Refer to the Decision-making Chart on pages 92–93. It will help you match your criteria against the jobs in question.

PRACTICE INTERVIEW QUESTIONS

Here are some questions you might be asked during your interview. Take time to think them through:

"Tell me about yourself." Talk about your strengths. Mention only what is relevant to the work you'll be doing. The company wants to know you can do the job. Give very specific examples from your past to prove you can.

"Why do you want to work here?" Let the interviewer know you've done your homework. Briefly tell them what impressed you about the company. Be enthusiastic. They are looking for someone who really *wants* to work there.

"Why should I hire you?" Here is where you highlight not only your qualifications but precisely how the company will benefit from what you have to offer. "My ability to motivate salespeople will have a direct impact on increasing the number of ads you will sell."

"What are your weaknesses?" List weaknesses that can be turned into strengths. "I am impatient, especially with mediocrity." "I am a real stickler for details."

"Why did you leave your last job?" Never ever criticize your former employer. Explain that you are changing jobs or fields to further your career. You can say your last job was routine, dead-ended, lacked training opportunities, or underutilized your strongest skills.

"What are your long-term goals?" Have a realistic and well-thought-out statement about what you hope to accomplish. You don't need to mention you'll want to be at another company or become more successful than your boss. Talk about internal as well as external rewards.

"Why were you out of work so long?" If there are any gaps on your resume, explain what you learned or accomplished during that period. Don't just say, "Well, I tried to find a job, but . . ." Try instead: "I spent the time reexamining my goals and decided . . ." "I took courses to expand my skills." "I volunteered to gain experience."

"Have you ever hired or fired anyone?" Questions like this are meant to determine the depth of your previous experience. If you have no experience in a certain area, you can convince the interviewer you are capable by relating similar experiences that demonstrate the skill set necessary. Have stories ready that illustrate your managerial skills.

QUESTIONS TO ASK AN EMPLOYMENT AGENCY

- Who are your clients?
- What is your track record?
- How many candidates did you place last year?
- How do you work with each candidate?
- What can I expect from you (progress reports, company lists)?
- How often will we talk?
- What level of candidate do you normally place?
- How much experience or knowledge do you have in my industry?
- Do you have a data base? A computerized system?
- Who is paying the fee?
- Do you network with other recruiters?

EMPLOYMENT INTERVIEW CHECKLIST

Complete this sheet prior to each interview. It will help you to organize your presentation and build your confidence for the interview.

Employer Information
(based on your research and networking activities)

Position being interviewed for: _____

Employer: _____ Department: _____

Interview location: _____
                    Street   City   State   Zip

Phone: _____

Date/Time of Interview: _____

Contact person(s): _____

Description of position being applied for: _____

_____

_____

Salary range: _____

Products/Services of Employer: _____

_____

Customer Profile: _____

_____

Competition: _____

_____

Public Image: _____

Recognized Problem Areas: _____

_____

Future Company Directions: _____

_____

_____

About Yourself
(based on your self-assessment and focusing exercises)

Skills and Abilities: _____

_____

Work/Personal Accomplishments: _____

_____

Job Criteria (prioritize): _____

_____

Anticipated Problem Areas: _____

_____

Questions to ask the Interviewer: _____

_____

Other Information: _____

_____

THE DECISION-MAKING CHART

If you are having difficulty deciding which job offer to accept, or whether a particular position would be right for you, this exercise will help you take an objective look at how well a particular job matches your criteria. Here's what you need to do:

1. Go back to the Summary Sheet on pages 29–30.
2. Take the items you circled as your priorities on that page and transfer them to the following chart. List each criterion separately in the spaces across the top of the chart.

Job Criteria for

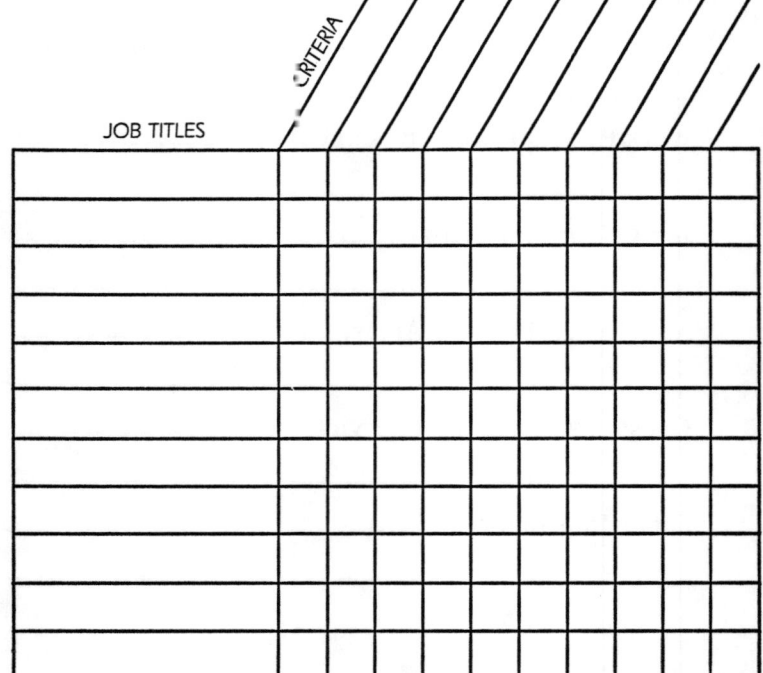

3. In the first column on the left-hand side, list the jobs you are considering. You can do this for one or more job titles.
4. Take the first job and, going across the sheet, put a number in each column—0 if the criteria are not present to 5 if they are very present. By doing this, you will be ranking the degree to which each of your criteria is satisfied in the job.
5. After you complete this chart, add up the points. The totals go in the far right column. Which choice ranks highest? Does this outcome confirm your instincts?

Decision Making

INCOME		ENVIRONMENT		INTERESTS		SKILLS		TASKS		TOTALS

7
SALARY
NEGOTIATION

Once you receive a job offer,
it's time to talk money.

For whatever reason—fear of rejection, lack of confidence, a wish to avoid conflict, or early conditioning—many people shy away from negotiating over salary. Instead, they hastily agree to whatever is offered or accept the first "no" as final. We don't want you to do that.

This chapter covers the main points of negotiation strategy and some techniques to help you in your hiring interview. Countless books and articles have been written to explain the important, often complex process of salary negotiation. This attention to the subject is well warranted. Considering the breadth of the topic, you might want to look through some of the books listed in the Suggested Reading list.

THE PROCESS

Let's start with a basic definition of negotiation. It is a give-and-take communication process that allows the parties with an interest in the outcome to reach a mutually satisfying agreement. Underline those last three words. The purpose of negotiation is to arrive at a point where all parties feel good about the results. Everyone wins something. No one is a loser. Beware of win-lose situations. Losers can get angry and nasty and seek revenge. You may not get everything you want, but the point is to come as close as you can without seriously antagonizng the other side.

PREPARATION

What goes into your head before you open your mouth is the foundation for a winning negotiation. In other words, your success will depend on how diligently you do your homework. If you have followed the previous steps outlined in this book, you have already laid much of the groundwork.

Preparation for salary negotiation should include the following:

Know the going rates in your field. Become familiar with salary ranges by asking direct questions during your informational interviews. In addition, talk to college placement centers, study want ads, call employment agencies, contact trade and professional associations, visit the public library, and read annual reports and company literature.

Understand your bargaining power. A job offer automatically gives you leverage. Obviously you have something the firm wants. Take a hard look at what you bring to the relationship. Then try to identify the employer's needs and determine the pressures he or she is under to fill the position.

Plan what you are going to say and how you will say it. Know the major points you want to make. Write them down if you like. Summarize the requirements of the job and match your skills and abilities to them. Develop convincing rebuttals to possible objections. Remember, the employer *expects* to bargain. Your task is to convince him or her that what you bring to the relationship is valuable and should be recompensed accordingly.

Practice ahead of time. Find a tape recorder or, better yet, a sparring partner to play devil's advocate and force you to think through answers to difficult questions. Also, mentally rehearse a successful encounter. Vividly imagine yourself achieving your goals.

Work on developing a positive attitude. As part of your homework, give yourself some pep talks. Attitude determines success. The most successful bargainers are those with the highest aspirations, who make the highest demands, and have the greatest respect for the other side. Remind yourself over and over again that the company would never have offered you the job if they didn't want you. Remember, too, that people tend to put a greater value on what they pay a high price for.

If the salary and benefits you are asking for are realistic, approach the negotiation with a cooperative, friendly, but persistent attitude. Let the employer know that you are willing to listen and evaluate all options in order to find a solution that is acceptable to you both.

If you are afraid that asking for more will cause the employer to lose interest in you, if you fear that never again will such an opportunity come your way, or if you take a "no" as a personal rejection, then you won't be able to negotiate very effectively. You'll be coming from a position of weakness instead of strength. Selling yourself short can lead to eventual frustration and dissatisfaction with the job.

A healthier attitude is believing that you are a valuable person with a lot to offer. You have the power to make an impact. The employer expects to bargain. You have everything to gain from the experience. (If nothing else, you gain the practice you need to perfect your negotiation skills).

THE PROCEDURE

Here are the most important factors in successful negotiating:

1. TIMING IS VERY IMPORTANT. Discuss salary only after you have been offered the job. In the course of the interview, should you be quizzed about salary requirements, you might respond: "I can't answer that without knowing more about the job."

2. DON'T UNDERESTIMATE THE POWER OF YOUR APPEARANCE. How you look and how you express yourself weigh heavily on the outcome. If you're seeking a professional position and commensurate salary, dress in a businesslike way.

3. LET THE INTERVIEWER MAKE THE FIRST OFFER. If asked what you feel you deserve, toss the ball back by responding, "What range did you have in mind?"

4. THINK IN TERMS OF SALARY RANGES. Identify a realistic figure and then ask for more so you have room to bargain. Career specialist Richard Bolles advises a range that "hooks" onto the one you've been given. If you know or estimate that they want to pay $30,000 to $36,000, you can counter the offer with "I believe my skills and experience are such that I should be in the $34,000 to $40,000 range." By positioning your minimum near the top of their maximum, you encourage them to go beyond their original offer, either now or in the future. If the employer won't budge, request a salary review three to six months after you've been hired.

5. DON'T NEGLECT FRINGE BENEFITS. These include insurance, pension plans, stock options, bonuses, vacations, sick leave, child care, and so on. These are valuable, negotiable items.

6. GET ALL AGREEMENTS IN WRITING. Include promises for future raises. Offer to draft the agreement yourself upon being offered the job.

NEGOTIATION TECHNIQUES

Negotiation techniques are limited only by your creativity, imagination, and knowledge. On the other hand, you may in fact be limited by the company's set policy and procedure, in terms of money, vacation time, sick leave, and the fringe benefits they offer. However, there are techniques whereby you can maximize your potential for gain and feel good about the bargaining.

Here are a few techniques you can use when discussing salary, promotion, or just about any negotiable topic:

Multiple-choice package. The more ways you give people to say "yes," the better your chance of getting what you want. Give them a choice of options rather than just a yes-or-no situation. You may request a larger starting salary, more fringe benefits, a higher performance bonus, or stock options.

Have patience. Instead of giving an on-the-spot answer, suggest taking time to think it over, or a "cooling off" period.

Put it on the back burner. If you get a rejection, suggest putting the whole thing on hold for a few days. People adjust slowly to new ideas.

Plant seeds. Keep planting hints and suggestions, over and over again. Instead of giving up if you don't get everything, chip away at little things and at least get a small share.

A slice at a time. Reach agreement on one item at a time and, before you know it, you may have the whole bundle or close to it.

Aim for the stars. Ask for more than you realistically can expect to get. This gives you room to bargain. But remember—pigs get fat; hogs get slaughtered!

Set deadlines. Establish time limits, but be flexible if you see progress.

Zip your lips. Silence is the most powerful tool you have. Don't fall into the trap of filling theirs. The smartest negotiators are those who don't jump in to fill a conversational gap.

Change your tone. Try shifting your style. This may range from subtly lowering or raising your voice to dramatically changing from a casual manner to a firmer one.

Include disposables. Ask for items that you are willing to throw away so that the other side will feel that you are making concessions.

Yes . . . and. Turn arguments to your advantage by agreeing with the other side, then overcoming the objection. Example: "I know I don't have a Ph.D., which the job description called for. Let me show you how I used that time in the field accumulating experience that will help you solve your problems."

Be the underdog. Show your weakness, beg ignorance. "I need your help."

Call in the experts. Quote statistics and the authorities to support your claim.

Create power. Get colleagues to go to work for you. Have them write letters of praise, put in a good word for you, etc.

Settle for less, temporarily. Accept a less acceptable solution for a specified amount of time. Example: "I'll take $25,000 for six months on the condition that it be raised to $30,000 if you're satisfied with my work."

Negotiation is not only important to win a good salary; your bargaining style will set the tone for the way you expect to be treated at work. What's more, your firmness as a negotiator indicates to your employer that you will act as firmly on his or her behalf once you get the job. In other words, your ability to strike a good deal argues well for your future performance on the job. With preparation, practice, and a winning attitude, you should be able to bargain with confidence and finesse, paving the way to a satisfying and rewarding work experience.

8
ON THE
JOB

No matter how terrific you are, if no one else
recognizes your contribution, you are in trouble.

Breathe a big sigh of relief and pat yourself on the
back. You got the job! The next step is to survive, thrive,
and achieve your goals. To accomplish this requires
that you plot your course artfully and politically. Most
job-hunting advice stops short of discussing how to begin a new job. Once you are hired, you are on your own.
But we feel that just as important as finding the right
job is keeping it.

More careers have been thwarted and ambitions
dashed by believing the timeworn myth that "if you
keep your nose to the grindstone and do your job well,
you will be justly rewarded." To succeed, top-quality
work is absolutely essential. But in today's fiercely competitive, fast-paced world, competence and hard work
in themselves no longer guarantee success.

Jodie's story is a good example. A marketing representative for a large manufacturing firm, Jodie met her
quotas, earned a few bonuses, worked long hard hours,
and took seminars to upgrade her skills. But no one
seemed to notice. Though others were promoted, she
stayed put—and couldn't understand it.

If you were to ask her, however, whether she social-
ized with anyone outside her immediate coworkers, or
if she ever volunteered for extra projects, she would
look at you in amazement. "Who has time?" she would

answer. As for documenting and communicating her ambitions and accomplishments, she assumed management was aware of those things.

The reverse behavior can be just as damaging. Joe, another client, was a brash overachiever. When he was hired away from a competing firm to become a new regional sales manager, his top priority was to take the division out of the red in the first six months. To do so required sweeping changes. He immediately cut expense allowances, readjusted the incentive schedule, and demanded monthly progress reports. Joe knew his people would groan, but, as he frequently told his superiors, it was the only way to improve production quickly. The results were disastrous. Productivity plummeted, along with morale. In an organization that valued team effort, Joe made a poor impression.

Both cases portray people who were hardworking, bright, ambitious, but who failed to assess their situations astutely. The key is to move slowly but strategically. The following suggestions have been compiled to help you get off on the right foot in your new job.

THE PROCEDURE

Take at least six months to orient yourself to the new job. If you move too fast, like Joe did, you risk making fatal mistakes. Drawing attention to yourself too early in the game could threaten coworkers and jeopardize your relationships. Begin quietly—but not passively, like Jodie. Study the organizational chart. Get to know the key departments and people. Try to discern who has clout. Power radiates through a web of informal relationships. Notice who lunches and socializes with whom. Get a sense of the corporate climate. In other words, play detective, snoop around, and size up the situation.

In addition, learn the goals and objectives of the company, your department, and your boss. Everything you do must mesh with those goals.

Set personal goals and establish priorities. Determine how high you want to climb and in what direction, so you can make critical yet fulfilling choices. Make sure your goals are "in sync" with the organization's philosophy. To ensure that your ideas are compatible, study the firm's long-range plans and talk to people whose judgment you respect. Role models and mentors can be particularly valuable. You can learn a lot simply by observing what works for them.

Communicate your goals. You must ask for what you want. It is unlikely your boss can read minds. It is up to you to make your ambitions known, tactfully and appropriately. However, be sure that you are reaching the person who has the power to make decisions. Recognizing the people with the *real* clout in the organization is important from the start.

Cultivate relationships with everyone. If we were pressed to limit ourselves to one piece of advice, this would be it. More than anything else, your relationships will determine your success. Studies indicate that personality problems, not lack of skill, account for more than 77 percent of all job losses. Make a concerted effort to be on good terms with *everyone* in the company, from the janitor to the president, and especially with the secretaries. Stay far, far away from conflict and cliques. And extend your network out into the field—with clients, other professionals, and even competitors.

Your network is of prime importance. Losing peer support is equivalent to committing professional suicide. You leave yourself exposed to some unpleasant surprises when you lose access to the grapevine.

From day one, get to know every employee even remotely connected to you. Find out about their jobs, preferences, and expectations. Ask for their support and offer yours: "If you have any problems and I can help, I hope you will come to me. At the same time, I hope I can count on your help and support." Build trust and rapport by helping people out, doing favors, and asking for advice.

Practice these techniques for reaching your goals:

1. Pay careful attention to your appearance. Your dress, materials, desk, and reports—all should say, "I am a professional." Your image can literally make or break your chances. Be scrupulous in your grooming.

2. Document your work. From the beginning, keep a portfolio that documents everything you do: ideas implemented, compliments received, seminars attended, suggestions given, ways you helped your boss, and so on. Such a list will be useful when you request a raise, promotion, or additional benefits and responsibilities. Use the chart on page 107 to track your accomplishments.

3. Showcase your skills and talents. No matter how terrific you are, if no one else recognizes your contribution, you're in trouble. Visibility is vital. Volunteer to do extra work. Whatever you promise, deliver more. This can mean taking the initiative to start a task force, showing up half an hour early for work, completing a project two weeks ahead of schedule.

4. Continually upgrade your skills. To increase your worth, take courses, go back for an advanced degree, attend conventions, read trade publications, and ask a lot of questions to update and expand your knowledge. Join professional organizations and look for opportunities to gain visibility, recognition, and leadership. Add these activities to your performance portfolio. You might even ask the organization's president or a committee chairperson to send your boss a letter of commendation for a job well done.

5. Respect the chain of command. It's risky to go over your boss's head. A pecking order prevails. You can try using the informal system to reach the higher-ups by giving other people the information you want to convey. Just be wary of being tagged as too politically cunning. You may have to wait longer to achieve your objectives, but you will avoid getting a damaging reputation as a manipulator.

6. Delegate. In your zealous effort to be a star performer, don't hoard all the responsibility or get buried under to-do piles. Overwork leads to burnout and robs you of valuable networking time. Moreover, making yourself indispensible, though it feeds your ego, could discourage your boss from losing you through promotion.

7. Find a mentor. Pick out a formal or informal mentor—someone who is successful and is willing to take you under his or her wing. This is one of the best strategies for learning the ropes and getting ahead. Some companies have mentor programs. You can ask someone to mentor or tutor you. Approach it as a project with a beginning and end, ask for specific help, and set up regular meeting times.

IN CONCLUSION

Jodie and Joe were able to salvage their jobs through career counseling. Each learned to apply the strategies discussed in this chapter to their situations.

Jodie concentrated on broadening her network by getting to know coworkers in other departments and identifying "rising stars" to serve as role models. She also began to use the work record on page 107 to document her accomplishments. It not only helped her when she applied for a promotion, it also boosted her self-confidence.

Joe, on the other hand, realized he needed to loosen up and listen more than dictate. He held weekly meetings to let everyone voice their ideas, complaints, and suggestions. He made sure his staff understood his reasons for policy changes. By taking the time to nurture relationships, Joe gained the support and respect of his people.

With careful and informed planning, you can lay the foundation for a winning future.

ON-THE-JOB ACTION PLAN

Just as you developed a written plan of action to research the job market, we suggest you follow a plan to establish goals for your career. However, keep in mind that a plan must be constantly evaluated and modified to adapt to changes that invariably occur.

Organization: _____

Current position: _____

What do I want to accomplish?

In the next six months to one year:

_____

_____

_____

In the next two to three years:

_____

_____

_____

How will I accomplish my goals (tools, strategies)?

_____

_____

_____

Individuals who could support and influence me:

_____

_____

_____

_____

Community resources I could use:

_____

_____

_____

Obstacles I may encounter:

_____

_____

_____

Strategies to overcome these obstacles:

_____

_____

_____

A TOOL FOR RECORDING YOUR ON-THE-JOB WORK EXPERIENCE

(for each volunteer or paid position)

The completion of this kind of record can be your first step in putting together a work portfolio. Use a different record for each job title or position you hold within your company and/or professional and community organization.

Job Title/Position: _____ Dates Held: _____

Agency or Organization: _____

Supervisor/Manager: _____

Brief job description of duties and responsibilities:

_____

_____

Skills and abilities used:

_____

_____

Accomplishments/recognition:

_____

_____

Likes and dislikes:

_____

_____

What I learned about myself:

_____

_____

9
NEGOTIATING
A RAISE

*Preparation is the key to success
and the best antidote for fear.*

As an employee with a good record, you now have a lot more bargaining power than when you first negotiated your salary. Still, asking for a raise is not easy. On the contrary, it takes a lot of courage. Our standard advice still holds: preparation is the key to success and the best antidote for fear. Figure out the right time to ask. Then assess your value to the company, inventory your skills, and evaluate your contributions.

The suggestions in Chapter 7 for negotiating a salary are applicable when you are requesting a raise. In addition, there are several more good strategies:

PREPARATION

Put together the following material:

1. A PORTFOLIO. In the previous chapter we suggested that you start a portfolio when you start the job. Include examples of your achievements, projects, performance appraisals, letters of recommendation, thank-you notes for jobs well done. (You can, if it's appropriate, solicit these from coworkers and colleagues.)

2. A LIST OF YOUR DUTIES. Highlight anything you've done beyond what is expected of you. Explain how your responsibilities have grown since your last pay increase.

3. A MARKET SURVEY. Find out what other firms are paying for the services you provide.

4. SPECIFIC EXAMPLES. List any cost-saving measures in which you helped the company earn or save time or money.

THE PROCEDURE

Prepare and practice in the same way you would for salary negotiation.

Timing is critical. Pick a time when the company is doing well and/or your boss has had a success and, psychologically speaking, may be feeling generous. Never approach your boss on hectic days. Mondays and Fridays are usually not good either. The best time is right after you've accomplished something important or been given a new responsibility. Some experts suggest that you request a raise a few weeks before a performance appraisal is scheduled.

Assess your boss's needs as well as the company's. Is your boss seeking prestige, personal power, and/or a promotion? If so, address these in your presentation.

Prepare an informal memo, either for mailing prior to the meeting or to be left at the end of the discussion, outlining your agenda. This note will help your boss remember the points you covered. It can also be conveniently passed on to anyone responsible for making final decisions.

Make an appointment with your boss. Don't barge in unexpectedly or mention it at the last moment.

Ask for a specific amount. Don't merely say you want a raise. Back up the request with references to your accomplishments. Consider asking for a bonus if a raise seems out of the question.

Project an efficient and competent image that says, "I can help you; I am worth it." Even if you feel like a quivering mass of Jell-O inside, fake it. Act as if you are cool, calm, and confident.

Listen carefully to objections. Chances are your boss is going to have some reservations. As long as objections remain unspoken, you will be unable to overcome them. Invite your boss to voice them. Don't become defensive or discouraged. Instead, counter them in a self-assured manner. (This is where practicing with a "sparring partner" will have helped.)

If successful, follow up with a memo: "This is what we agreed on."

If unsuccessful, find out why. Ask your boss why he or she is turning you down and use the feedback to adjust your objectives, activities, and perhaps your approach. Ask for review in a certain number of months.

WARNING

Never threaten to quit if you don't get a raise—unless you mean it. That approach will antagonize your boss and work against you. Instead, emphasize how much you enjoy your job and the company, and then bring up the issue of adjusting your salary.

Don't appeal to your boss with the plea "I need a raise. I've got two kids in college." Needing more money isn't reason enough to get it. You must show that you deserve a raise based on your contribution. Always support your request with facts.

Don't apologize, appear unsure, or say how difficult it is for you to talk about money. These are sure turnoffs and will make it too easy for your boss to refuse you.

One of the major reasons people are underpaid is that they are simply afraid to ask for what they deserve. If you're nervous (and most people are), ask yourself what is the worst thing that could happen if your boss said no. If you prepare you case thoroughly and understand the principles of negotiating, you have laid the foundation that will produce results—if not this time, then perhaps the next.

10
WORK ALTERNATIVES

Consider these alternatives not only as
viable options to traditional employment
but as a way to get your foot in the door.

Up to now we have been discussing the typical nine-to-five kind of job. However, you have other choices: temporary work, part-time, flextime, job sharing, volunteerism, internship, and self-employment.

These alternatives are viable options to traditional employment. They are also a way to get your foot in the door, gain experience, explore new fields and organizations, brush up on skills, and establish credentials. What's more, they provide you with an income while you look for a job.

WHERE TO FIND WORK ALTERNATIVES

Work options are becoming more and more popular with companies. They allow employers to add staff as needed, retain valued employees who want more flexibility, and hold payroll costs down. Of course, some businesses are more responsive to nontraditional arrangements than others. These include companies that are:

- small and may not need full-time help;
- innovative and receptive to new ideas;

- nonprofit organizations;
- employing free-lancers;
- affected by peak periods (farms, tax firms, mail-order houses);
- large with high turnover and/or project-oriented tasks;
- having layoffs or budget cuts.

The fact is, any employer may be a candidate. However, you may have to work harder at selling the idea to some more than others.

Let's take a closer look at your options:

TEMPORARY WORK

When businesses find themselves needing extra help, but do not want to hire permanent staff, they often turn to temporary employees. You can sign up with a temporary agency. Ask your friends which ones they've used. You'll also find them listed in the yellow pages and newspaper want ads. The way the system works is that the agency becomes your employer. It pays you a salary, benefits, and deducts taxes. And it sends you out on assignments.

If you can type you can always find a temporary position. But beyond clerical work, there is a tremendous demand for just about any skill or profession. There are temporary executives, lawyers, medical personnel, computer specialists, writers, accountants. . . . You name it, there is a need for temporary labor.

Temporary work provides an opportunity to get inside a company and be there when job openings are posted. Often these result in permanent positions. What's more, some people, wanting flexibility in their profession or their hours, make a career of being a temporary worker.

Part-time, Flextime, and Job Sharing
Over the past decade, many companies have begun experimenting with creative work alternatives. Three options gaining popularity are:

112

Part-time work. The latest census shows that one out of every six persons is employed part-time, and the number of part-time jobs is growing at double the rate of full-time positions. While the wages are usually lower and fringe benefits lacking, the situation is changing. Many people, in all fields, are negotiating for professional part-time status.

Flextime. An alternative to the rigid nine-to-five day, the flexible work schedule gives you more leeway in the hours you work. You can agree, for example, to be at the office during a core period of, say 10 A.M. to 2 P.M., and then you can determine when you work the other four hours.

Job sharing. This is an arrangement where usually two people agree to share the responsibilities, salary, and benefits of one job. In effect, one full-time job becomes two part-time jobs.

You may need to convince the employer to let you arrange an alternative work schedule. Just like interviewing for a job, the key will be to show your boss the advantages of such an arrangement—to them and the company. Advantages could include: a way to cover peak periods of business, reduce overtime, increase productivity, generate new options for older employees and for parents of young children, reduce absenteeism, retain valued employees, and offset layoffs.

To help you in your efforts to set up an alternative situation in your present job or in a new one, we suggest the following steps:

1. LEARN ABOUT THE DIFFERENT OPTIONS TO SEE WHICH ONES WOULD BEST MEET YOUR NEEDS AND GOALS.
- Read books and periodicals (see Suggested Reading list at back of book).
- Contact the Society for Work Options (c/o Focus, 509 Tenth Avenue East, Seattle, Washington 98102, 206-329-7918) for information on work options in your locale.
- Talk to others who have been involved with work

alternatives, either as an employee or supervisor. (Use your informational interviews to learn more about this.)

- Collect facts and statistics that reinforce the advantages of these options.

2. RESEARCH PARTICULAR INDUSTRIES AND COMPANIES THAT INTEREST YOU.

- Make sure you understand the nature of the business before you propose any changes.
- Find out the employer's personnel needs.

3. KNOW YOURSELF AND YOUR SKILLS.

- Identify your personal and functional skills that meet the employer's needs.

4. DEVELOP A WRITTEN PROPOSAL TO PRESENT TO THE EMPLOYER.

- Describe your purpose in wanting a work alternative.
- List the benefits—how your proposed plan will meet their needs.
- Work out a proposed schedule—that is, a list of tasks and responsibilities required to do the job, how you will split those tasks, who will do what, when they will get done, and the specific hours you will work.
- Suggest a prorated wage and benefits package.

5. SELL YOUR IDEA TO THE EMPLOYER.

- Use the techniques described in earlier chapters for interviewing and negotiating.
- Practice your presentation with a friend.

Be aware that many companies will be reluctant to risk a new staffing plan. All the more reason to thoroughly research, prepare, and sell the benefits of your plan to the company. Making the company's administration knowledgeable about creative work alternatives may be step one.

VOLUNTEER WORK AND INTERNSHIP

Career changers and college graduates face a catch-22: to get a job you need experience. But how do you get experience if you can't get a job? The answer might be volunteering. For almost any skill you want to develop, there is a volunteer position that will help you learn it: media relations, public speaking, group facilitating, accounting, computers, acting, legal work—the list is endless. Volunteer work often leads to paid employment, and should be treated with the same professionalism. Keep records, maintain a portfolio, obtain letters of recommendation and evaluation forms, and, by all means, include your volunteer experience under employment history in your resume.

Look in the Resource Guide for volunteer centers. Or find an organization and offer your time. Volunteer work tends to be in nonprofit organizations and is, of course, not paid for.

There is a way, however, to "volunteer" for profit-oriented companies. In those instances, it is called internship. Many large companies, and even smaller ones, offer formal internship programs. They are often, but certainly not always, filled by students who take a semester off to get practical experience along with college credit. Anyone can apply for an internship. And, in fact, some programs pay a small salary. Normally an internship requires some basic knowledge and prior experience. Some schools will set up internships but often it is up to you to initiate the action. Simply call the places you would like to work at and offer your services as an intern.

ENTREPRENEURSHIP

Starting a business is a popular American dream. And, in these days of corporate turmoil, this option is becoming more and more common and possible.

Over 1.1 million people a year are leaving companies

to start a business. They are lured by the opportunity to control their own time, test their skills, get paid directly, do what they really love doing, and create more flexibility to combine child rearing with career.

Nevertheless, we must warn you. Building your own business is no quick cure for the job-hunt jitters. The time and energy necessary to set up shop will make job hunting look like a vacation. The approach is basically the same: advance preparation, planning, research, and networking. Moreover, in the first one to three years, you may work longer hours (expect twelve-hour days) and earn less than your salaried friends.

Financial assistance is frustratingly difficult to obtain, some say impossible without a rich relative or generous friend. To further dampen your spirits, the Small Business Administration claims that 50 to 80 percent of all new ventures fail within the first five years.

Still, the rewards of self-employment can certainly outshine the negatives if you do your homework. The key, says San Francisco small business expert Paul Terry, is to plan, be persistent, learn as you grow, and, perhaps most important, understand and be able to work with numbers. "Entrepreneurs are not afraid to risk," says Terry. "But the successful ones are actually risk avoiders. They minimize risks by doing their homework."

We have briefly sketched out the basic steps you need to consider in setting up a business. This is simply meant to be a checklist. For more help and information, consult the Resource Guide and the Suggested Reading list.

1. Learn all you can about yourself, your field, and business ownership in general. That means:
- Discuss your ideas with friends, colleagues, and authorities in your field. Keep notes.
- Talk to business owners (any business will do). Have a list of common questions.
- Study the competition, including firms in other geographical locations. Do comparisons.
- Attend workshops, seminars, conventions. The

Small Business Administration and local colleges offer frequent classes.
- Read books, journals, newspapers.
- Join a professional network of other business owners to give you motivation and support.

2. Find a need and fill it. Pick a field you know and love.
- Pay close attention to the economy and current events so you can respond quickly when change occurs.
- Stay informed on industry changes and growth.
- Carefully investigate your idea and test it part-time, if possible.

3. Examine all options. Weigh the pitfalls against the pluses. For example, will you:
- Start your own shop or office or work out of your home?
- Acquire a going firm or a franchise or start from scratch?
- Moonlight until you can go full-time or plunge right in?
- Take on a partnership or become sole owner?

4. Develop a comprehensive written plan before you start. This plan is your road map or itinerary. It will keep you on track.
- Describe your service or product.
- State your purpose, goals, and objectives.
- Develop strategies: marketing, pricing, expansion.
- Pinpoint your expected sources of clients, customers, and project income.
- Identify and compare your competition, present and potential.
- Describe the advantages of using your business over the competition.
- Carefully assess how much money you will need to get started and survive for the first year.
- Develop a plan for raising that money and paying it back.

5. Stop here. . . . Make sure all these variables make sense and are realistic and attainable. Show your plans to business friends and advisors.

6. Get experience.
- Take a temporary job in the industry.
- Volunteer in the field.
- Enroll in relevant training programs or college courses. Since 90 percent of all failures are due to managerial incompetence, be sure to take a management course. Also, take accounting courses. You need to keep close tabs on your financial information.

7. Employ professionals.
- An accountant and a lawyer are a must.
- A banker and insurance agent are important.
- Using paid consultants with special expertise may be a wise investment.
- Know your limits and delegate. Hire help if you need it.

8. Believe with all your heart you will succeed!
WARNING: You will be confronted with many roadblocks, including people who will tell you your idea will never fly. This is important for you to hear. Confronting these pessimists will force you to test your convictions and level of commitment. Realize that they are only people with opinions, not prophets with psychic powers. If they succeed in discouraging you, be grateful. Your commitment was not strong enough to make it work. If, on the other hand, you are determined to succeed, you probably will. If you have done your homework, made a realistic assessment of the potential for success, and passionately believe you can succeed, then by all means *do it*. And good luck.

ONE FINAL WORD

We have attempted to show you a methodical approach to finding a job. Our hope is that you not only become happily employed but enjoy the journey along the way. In the preceding chapters we have taken you step-by-step through this journey—from getting focused to getting hired. There are, however, some additional points we would like to mention. They can make a big difference in your efforts to becoming happily employed.

First, you have within you the power to shape your future simply by focusing on what you want to happen. It might sound farfetched, but studies in the fields of science, medicine, and sports have shown that by creating vivid mental pictures of desired results, you can considerably influence the outcome of events.

"Things we visualize, even though unlikely, begin to happen with increasing frequency," wrote Menninger Foundation research scientist Elmer Green in his book, *Beyond Biofeedback*. In other words, by visualizing yourself in your ideal job, you can actually increase your chances for getting it. (What you need to watch out for, however, is unknowingly focusing on the negative as so many people do.)

You can further swing the odds in your favor by repeating, over and over again, like a mantra, positive statements about success. "I am confident that I will achieve whatever I set out to do." "I am happily employed doing what I love." These affirmations, over a period of time, will actually reprogram your subconscious mind and propel you toward your goals.

Another important point to be made: you are not only powerful, you are wise. Trust your hunches. If you've done the footwork we have suggested and are armed with good solid information, your best guide will always be your own inner signals. In your heart, you know better than anyone else what you want and what you need. Listen to your intuition. Trust it.

With all the instruction, advice, and guidance we have offered, it all boils down to *you*. You must do the work to realize your goals. By taking the time to figure out what you want, talking to other people, researching possibilities, and using all the resources available, you are well on the road to success. It is a rocky road to be sure. You are bound to run into patches of fog and moments of utter darkness. At times, you are going to have to push yourself to make one more phone call, to risk failure and endure rejection without personalizing it, and to keep up the faith when there is no end in sight.

Throughout these pages, we have tried to be your guide and, most of all, keep you going through the tough times. To that end, we would like to leave you with a short parable as a way to sum up how we see the process working:

> When nothing seems to help, go and look at the stonecutter hammering away at his rock perhaps a hundred times without as much as a crack showing in it. Yet at the hundredth and first blow it will split in two, and you know it was not that blow that did it, but all that had gone before.

Every step you take brings you that much closer to knowing the joy of using your talents, doing work that matters to you, and being amply rewarded for your accomplishments. That is the joy of being happily employed.

DALLAS–
FORT WORTH
AREA
JOB HUNTER'S
RESOURCE GUIDE

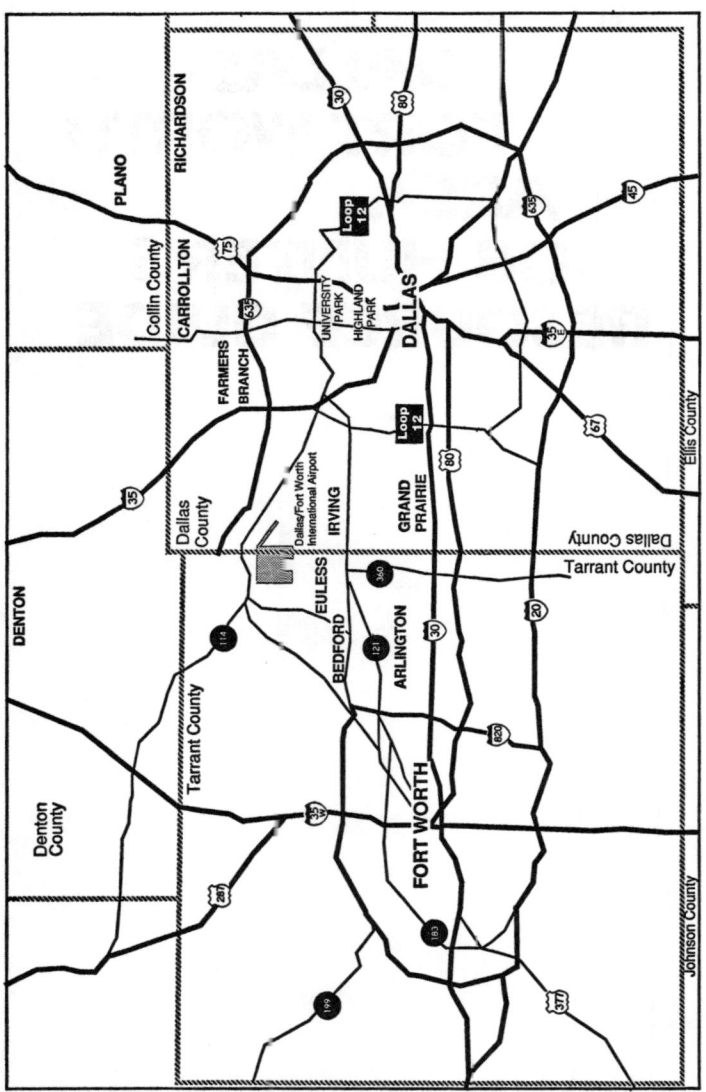

Credit: Lisa J. Smith

CONTENTS

This Resource Guide is designed to introduce you to some of the area's most valuable resources for finding a job as well as enhancing your career. Key industries and employers, career exploration and training resources, counseling and job referral services, professional networks and resources for the growing entrepreneur sector are all included.

In addition, we have listed some lesser-known services and hard-to-find information. For example, do you know that many government agencies, employers, and professional organizations have employment "hot lines" that give specifics on available jobs? Or that there are many directories to help you identify potential employers?

The outlook for employment in the Dallas–Fort Worth area is especially strong in high technology, telecommunications, transportation, and health care. However, be aware that many people in Dallas and Fort Worth are assessing their careers and job opportunities because of an upheaval in what were once growth industries—financial institutions, real estate, and oil and gas. While most economists believe the state's economy is on the way back up, many employers are being cautious in their hiring and some displaced workers are still looking for jobs. Job hunters may find themselves competing for positions along with unemployed bank vice presidents, geologists, and retail store managers who lost their jobs during the area's numerous business reshufflings.

A unique advantage of this area, however, is that the two-city market gives job hunters a wide range of industries, corporate cultures, and life-styles to choose from. Dallas and Fort Worth are two distinct places with distinct personalities and career opportunities. With a population of about 961,000, Dallas is more than twice as large as Fort Worth. It is the more cosmopolitan city, fancying itself as the New York of the Southwest. The city is the state's financial center, although its banks and savings and loans have undergone a major restructuring in recent years.

Dallas is mainly white collar, with a more formal corporate culture than Fort Worth except in creative businesses and "shirtsleeves" industries like high technology. You'll hear lots of different accents in Dallas. Corporate relocations have transplanted workers to the area from all over the United States.

As its traditional major industries have faltered in recent years, Dallas's leadership has been undergoing a transition. A younger, more entrepreneurial style of leadership is emerging, although business interests still heavily influence local government.

Commuting—and sitting in traffic—is a way of life for many residents. Many people work in Dallas but live in the fast-growing suburbs. To the north these include Richardson, Plano, and Carrollton; in the southwest, Duncanville, DeSoto, and Cedar Hill. Residents also commute from all over the area to Richardson and Plano, seats of the area's high-technology and telecommunications industries. An automobile with a cellular telephone is the preferred way of getting around, although the regional transit authority is beginning to improve bus service to outlying suburbs.

In addition to some of the drawbacks of big-city life, Dallas also has some of the advantages: major-league sports teams, museums, restaurants, theaters and good shopping malls, tourist attractions such as the John F. Kennedy Memorial Plaza and Sixth-Floor Exhibit, the Arts District—to say nothing of Southfork Ranch of television's *Dallas*.

Fort Worth, in contrast, prides itself on being "where the West begins." Locals still call the city "Cowtown," referring to Fort Worth's heritage as a major cattle town on Chisholm Trail, and attractions such as the Stockyards area and events such as the annual Southwestern Exposition and Livestock Show reinforce the image.

Fort Worth offers an informal corporate culture. It's not unusual to see businessmen or even city officials strolling the streets of downtown wearing Western suits and bolo ties or blue jeans and cowboy boots.

Many economists believe Fort Worth fared better during the state's economic recession because of the heavy federal spending in the city. Fort Worth's share of defense dollars is among the highest in the nation, with major defense plants including General Dynamics, Bell Helicopter Textron, and Carswell Air Force Base.

Fort Worth also offers a more laid-back life-style. In fact, *Newsweek* magazine recently named Fort Worth one of the best places to live and work, citing the city's parks (second in acreage only to Chicago), quality art museums, lack of traffic congestion, and the preservation of its Western heritage.

Whether you decide to live and work in Dallas or Fort Worth, this Resource Guide is designed to stimulate your imagination and show you the range of job and career possibilities in the area.

CAREER INFORMATION, COUNSELING, AND JOB REFERRAL RESOURCES

There really are two types of people who do career counseling. There are people who do testing and then come up with suggestions on vocations to explore. When you're talking about how to get a job, you need to go another step. You need help identifying potential employers in your area, somebody who knows the economy in Dallas–Fort Worth. When you need a job, you need someone with good contacts in the area.

"The type of career counselor that's right for the job seeker really depends on if a person needs to get a job or needs help deciding what they want to do."

Mary Holdcroft, president, Career Management Resources

Now that you're more familiar with the Dallas–Fort Worth area and its variety of opportunities, where do you start looking for a job or exploring a career direction?

This chapter identifies some of the area's best sources for career information, counseling, and job referrals.

The area's large community college system and universities have professional career counselors and placement specialists to help students and alumni, and some of them are expanding their services to the community.

Government agencies have traditionally been a rich source of job listings. They also are becoming more sophisticated in their services, offering seminars and workshops to help people conduct a self-directed job search.

Private career counselors go a step beyond most publicly available services, offering individualized, specialized attention to help steer you on the right career path—for a fee.

NONPROFIT ORGANIZATIONS

Several nonprofit organizations offer comprehensive career services. Others provide job listings or support groups or seminars for job seekers. Their services are free unless noted in the following listing.

Many organizations target special interest groups or operate in a limited geographic area, so it's best to ask on the telephone about any restrictions before visiting their offices.

ARLINGTON

Women's Center of Tarrant
  County
Arlington Branch
401 W. Sanford St., Suite 1200
Arlington, TX 76011
(817) 548-1663
Job search club, job referral and placement, employment counseling and interview workshops, resume assistance, mentor network, information on skill training. Open to men and women.

DALLAS

Aptitude Inventory Measurement Services (AIMS)
5220 McKinney Ave., Suite 30
Dallas, TX 75205
(214) 741-2430
Career and college counseling, specializing in new college graduates and mid-life job changes. Fee charged.

Citizens Development Center
8800 Ambassador Row
Dallas, TX 75247
(214) 637-2911
Workshops, testing, employment preparation, interviewing techniques for disabled persons. Fee for work adjustment training.

Dallas Alliance of Businessmen
4501 Lemmon Ave.
Dallas, TX 75219
(214) 528-6130
Employment counseling and job listings for general public and low-income persons.

Dallas Center for Independent
  Living
8625 King George Dr., Suite
  210
Dallas, TX 75235
(214) 631-6900
Career counseling, job listings, workshops, resource library, resume assistance, interviewing techniques for disabled.

Dallas Inter-Tribal Center
209 E. Jefferson Blvd.
Dallas, TX 75203
(214) 941-6535
Career counseling, job training, testing, resume assistance, interviewing techniques, and job listings for American Indians only.

Dallas Urban League
2121 Main St., Suite 410
Dallas, TX 75201
(214) 747-4734
Employment and career counseling, resume assistance, interviewing, job placement for minority groups and economically disadvantaged.

Forty Plus
13601 Preston Rd.
Dallas, TX 75240
(214) 991-9917
Outplacement, support groups, testing and skill assessment, workshops, resume assistance, referrals, interviewing skills. Must be more than forty years old. Application fee, membership dues, and exit fee.

Jewish Family Service
7800 Northaven Rd., Suite B
Dallas, TX 75230
(214) 696-6400

*Assessment, counseling, job
placement, resume assistance,
and interviewing skills for Jewish
community, handicapped, senior
citizens, displaced workers, new
Americans with a language bar-
rier. Sliding fee based on income.*

Project Link/Mainstream Inc.
2121 San Jacinto St., Suite 855
Dallas, TX 75201
(214) 696-0118

*Career counseling, resume assis-
tance, interviewing techniques,
job listings, job search books for
mentally and physically disabled.*

Women's Center of Dallas
3505 Turtle Creek Blvd.,
  Suite 103
Dallas, TX 75219
(214) 521-9606

*Sponsors WISER program
(Women in Search of Executive
Responsibilities). Compiles information on displaced women executives and maintains a data
base available to employers.*

Women's Resource Center
Young Women's Christian
  Association
4621 Ross Ave.
Dallas, TX 75204
(214) 821-9595

*Career planning, occupational
testing, job-hunting strategies,
networking and resume assistance for women. Fee charged.*

FORT WORTH

Women's Center of Tarrant
  County Inc.
1723 Hemphill St.
Fort Worth, TX 76110
(817) 927-4050

*Job search clubs, job bank,
placement, counseling, interview
workshops, resume assistance,
network of mentors, information
on skill training. Open to men
and women. Nominal fee based
on ability to pay.*

IRVING

Johnson O'Connor Research
  Foundation Inc.
Human Engineering Laboratory
4950 N. O'Connor Rd.,
  Suite 250
Irving, TX 75062
(214) 541-0650 or metro
  (214) 791-0330

*Assessment and testing for people
fourteen years and older. Recommended for students and persons
changing careers, returning to
job market, retiring, or other
transitions. Fee charged.*

COMMUNITY COLLEGES
AND UNIVERSITIES

Community colleges and universities can be very helpful
whether you want to explore your interests and aptitudes,
change careers, or find out more about the local job market.
Some Dallas–Fort Worth area colleges allow only students
and alumni to use their career services, but others offer these
services to the public. Though they may charge a fee, it is
usually much lower than a private career counselor's.

  Job listings frequently are on a computer, and several universities administer computerized testing and interest as-

sessment programs. The seven colleges in the Dallas County Community College District share a computerized job bank that contains updated listings of jobs related to courses taught at the colleges. In addition to career counselors, each college has a placement coordinator.

It takes enrollment in only one class at the community colleges to qualify as a student, so it may be worthwhile to take a course and at the same time gain access to career counseling and placement services. Some universities also have reciprocal programs, so an alumnus from an institution outside the area may be able to use a local university's career counseling and placement services.

Check with the career counseling services at area institutions for further information on their programs. Many have brochures they can mail you explaining their services and restrictions in greater detail.

ARLINGTON

The University of Texas at Arlington
Counseling and Career Development Center
800 S. Cooper St.
Box 19156
Arlington, TX 76019
(817) 273-3671

Career and life planning, some testing, resource library, job listings, annual job fair for UTA students and alumni. Skill-building seminars occasionally open to the public for a fee.

DALLAS

El Centro Community College
Counseling Center
Main and Lamar Sts.
Dallas, TX 75202-3604
(214) 746-2084

Career counseling, testing, computerized job bank, resource library, and job placement free to students and alumni. Nonstudents pay fee for tests.

Mountain View Community College
Career Center
4849 W. Illinois Ave.
Dallas, TX 75211
(214) 333-8606

Counseling, testing, resource library, and placement services free to students and alumni. Workshops and seminars open to the public free.

Richland Community College
12800 Abrams Rd.
Dallas, TX 75243
(214) 238-6020

Largest and most publicly accessible career counseling program in the Dallas community college system. Free counseling, testing, resume assistance, and resource library for students and alumni. Recently expanded community program offers package of services for a fee.

Southern Methodist University
Career Center
P.O. Box 256
Dallas, TX 75275
(214) 692-2266

Career counseling, computerized assessment, job listings, resume assistance, job fairs free to students. Alumni pay fee. Reciprocity agreements. Class on changing careers offered to public through continuing education program.

130

DENTON

Texas Woman's University
Career and Employment
  Services
P.O. Box 22939, TWU Station
Denton, TX 76204
(817) 898-2950
Career counseling, testing, placement, and career library free to students and alumni. Students completing twelve credit hours can receive job listings by mail, resume assistance, interviewing and job search tips.

University of North Texas
Career Planning and Placement
  Services
P.O. Box 13378
Denton, TX 76203
Metro (817) 267-3731 or
  (817) 565-2105
Counseling, placement, job referrals and listings, computerized job matching service, resource library, interviewing techniques, and resume assistance free to students and alumni. Job search seminars open to public.

FARMERS BRANCH

Brookhaven Community
  College
Counseling Center
3939 Valley View La.
Farmers Branch, TX 75244
(214) 620-4830
Counseling, testing, and placement services offered free to students and alumni. Adult Center sponsors free brown-bag lunch seminars on topics such as interviewing and resume writing.

FORT WORTH

Tarrant County Junior College ·
Northwest Campus
Counseling and Career Placement Services
4801 Marine Creek Pkwy.
Fort Worth, TX 76179
(817) 232-7788
Career counseling, workshops, academic advisement, training

and consultation, testing, resource library, on-campus interviewing, placement free to students and alumni of any TCJC campus.

Texas Christian University
Career Planning and Placement
  Center
2800 S. University Dr.
Fort Worth, TX 76129
(817) 921-7860
Career counseling, testing, placement, resource library, job listings, on-campus interviewing, job fairs free to students and alumni. Weekly bulletin The Career Connection *lists job openings for students and alumni.*

Texas Wesleyan College
1201 Wesleyan Dr.
Fort Worth, TX 76105
Metro (817) 429-8224 or
  (817) 531-4432
Career counseling, testing, and interviewing assistance free to students and alumni only.

IRVING

North Lake Community College
Career Planning and Placement
  Office
5001 N. MacArthur Blvd.
Irving, TX 75062
(214) 659-5218
Career counseling and placement free to students and alumni. Brown-bag seminars on career topics free and open to the public.

University of Dallas
Career Development Center
1845 E. Northgate Dr.
Irving, TX 75062-4799
(214) 721-5000
Career counseling, career library, resume writing, videotaped mock interviews, job search strategy planning, on-campus interviews, workshops for students and alumni. Class offered on career decision making.

131

LANCASTER

Cedar Valley Community
  College
3030 N. Dallas Ave.
Lancaster, TX 75134
(214) 372-8262
*Career counseling, testing, and
job placement free to students.
Testing available to nonstudents
for a fee. Job listings available to
public.*

MESQUITE

Eastfield Community College
Center for Student Success
3737 Motley Dr.
Mesquite, TX 75150
(214) 324-7039
*Career counseling, computerized
testing, job listings, job fairs, employment seminars, and career li-*
*brary free to students and alumni
of any Dallas County community
college. Nonstudents pay fee for
computerized testing.*

RICHARDSON

The University of Texas at
  Dallas
Office of Career Planning and
  Placement
2601 Floyd Rd.
P.O. Box 830688, MC16
Richardson, TX 75083-0688
(214) 690-2943
*Career counseling, testing, job re-
ferrals, on-campus recruiting, career library, job fairs, and
seminars available to students
and alumni only. Students pay
fee to register with office. Alumni
pay fee for testing and career
counseling.*

GOVERNMENT AGENCIES

Texas Employment Commission

Any discussion of government agencies has to start with the
Texas Employment Commission. The TEC is one of the best
resources for obtaining job information and acquiring the
skills for effective job searching. The agency's services are
free and open to anyone—whether employed or unemployed,
living in the state or outside it.

Twenty TEC offices in Dallas, Fort Worth, and nearby communities provide job listings, process claims for unemployment insurance, and compile job market data that the state
will use in making decisions about employment and training.
The TEC's job listings are the most comprehensive in the
state. The majority are for full-time positions. Professional,
clerical, and service positions account for the largest percentage of jobs in the listing.

TEC offices also offer testing for skills and aptitudes, some
counseling and referrals to other agencies, particularly those
participating in the federal Job Training Partnership Act.

In recent years some offices have added a Job Search Seminar program that gives unemployed participants the skills
they need to find jobs on their own and get back to work. The
half-day seminars are held at the downtown Dallas and Fort
Worth offices, and in Richardson. They focus on goal setting,

resume writing, and interviewing techniques. A resource room with job search books, directories, and other publications is also available to participants.

Listed below are some of the area TEC office locations.

ARLINGTON

979 N. Cooper St.
Arlington, TX 76012
(817) 265-8431

CARROLLTON

1718 Trinity Valley Dr.
Carrollton, TX 75006
(214) 620-1351

DALLAS

Kessler Hills
1050 N. Westmoreland Rd.,
  Suite 316
Dallas, TX 75211
(214) 330-5183

Lancaster-Kiest
408 Lancaster-Kiest Shopping
  Center
Dallas, TX 75216
(214) 372-1471

Martin Luther King Commu-
  nity Center
2922 MLK Jr. Blvd.
Dallas, TX 75215
(214) 421-2460

Seminar and Testing Center
2808 Fairmount St.
Dallas, TX 75201
(214) 871-8800

District Office
8300 John Carpenter Fwy.
Dallas, TX 75356
(214) 631-6050

DENTON

510 Interstate 35 E-North
Denton, TX 76202
(817) 382-6712

FORT WORTH

301 W. 13th St.
Fort Worth, TX 76101
(817) 335-5111

GARLAND

217 10th St.
Garland, TX 75046
(214) 276-8361

GRAND PRAIRIE

202 W. Hwy. 303
Grand Prairie, TX 75053
(214) 264-5881

HURST/MID-CITIES

1225 Precinct Line Rd.
Hurst, TX 76053
(817) 282-9845

IRVING

201 S. Rogers St.
Irving, TX 75015
(214) 254-9135

MESQUITE

4625 Eastover Dr.
Mesquite, TX 75149
(214) 388-5840

RICHARDSON/PLANO

1222 E. Arapaho Rd.
Richardson, TX 75083
(214) 234-5391

Other Government Agencies

Besides the TEC, city and county agencies also offer a range of employment and career services, many targeted to specific groups. Check with these organizations before you visit them for any restrictions on eligibility.

DALLAS

Dallas County Community Action Committee Inc.
2121 Main St., Suite 208
Dallas, TX 75201
(214) 939-0588
Job placement, career counseling, resume and job correspondence assistance, testing, interviewing skills, job listings for economically disadvantaged.

SER Jobs for Progress Inc.
2514 Harry Hines Blvd.
Dallas, TX 75201
(214) 871-7575
Training, GED classes, English classes, job placement, and job listings for Spanish-speaking persons in Dallas County.

Senior Employment Program
2727 Inwood Rd., Suite 100
Dallas, TX 75235
(214) 956-8704
Job placement and job listings for Dallas County residents over fifty-five.

Texas Rehabilitation
  Commission
2415 W. Northwest Hwy.,
  Suite 102
Dallas, TX 75220
(214) 387-8695
Job training, placement, evaluation, and follow-up for disabled.

FORT WORTH

Masters Program
712 W. Magnolia Ave.
Fort Worth, TX 76104
(817) 870-8798
Assistance in locating part-time and full-time work training in community service or nonprofit organizations, assistance in job search, and resume preparation for persons fifty-five or older.

The Working Connection
440 S. Main St.
Fort Worth, TX 76104
(817) 870-8790
Assessment, employment preparation and motivation, job training, job placement, and job club for handicapped or economically disadvantaged.

GARLAND

City of Garland Neighborhood
  Service Center
701 Clark St.
Garland, TX 75040
(214) 205-3310
Job referrals.

CAREER CONSULTANTS

Whether you want to find out more about yourself and what career suits your personality, or you want a specific job in a specific industry, private career consultants can help in the search. Firms and fees vary greatly, so shop around for the right person at the right price.

Career consultants, usually psychologists, administer tests to determine your interests and skills. Many will provide consultations and reports to help you assess the kind of career that would best suit your personality and life-style.

Other consultants emphasize the job search itself, providing assistance with resumes and cover letters, giving pointers on interviewing, and offering solid job leads and even placement. Still others are "full-service" career consultants, offering individualized testing and job search assistance, providing support along the way, furnishing books, directories, and information on local employers, and even negotiating your salary with a potential employer.

The best way to check which career consultant is right for you is a referral by a friend or acquaintance who has used a particular firm. Ask around. If you don't know anyone who can give you a reference, call the firm directly and talk to one of the principals. Any reputable firm should be happy to explain its services over the phone or send you a brochure. Many firms offer a free initial consultation.

Credentials are also a guide to a career counselor's approach and experience. Many career counselors in the area have master's degrees in education or counseling, and several have doctorates. Some counselors have gone the extra step of becoming Licensed Professional Counselors, or LPCs.

The Texas Department of Labor and Standards recently began requiring career counselors to obtain a "career counseling service certificate of authority." The certification entails paying a fee, posting a bond that would protect clients in case the business fails, and having a certified public accountant approve the counseling firm's finances. The law is still relatively new, however, and many career consultants haven't yet received the certification. For those that are certified, "CCC" appears after their name in the listing that follows.

If you're not sure about a particular firm's services, check with the Better Business Bureau in either Dallas or Fort Worth to see if they've had any complaints from clients.

The following listing of career counselors reflects the variety of career counseling available in the Dallas–Fort Worth area. Inclusion does not imply endorsement. Firms were selected on the basis of the services they offer and their geographic locations. Most of the firms listed provide consultations and some level of skill and interest assessment and testing, so those services aren't noted unless they're specialties. The quoted remarks at the bottom of each entry are from the firm itself.

ARLINGTON

William M. Helton, Jr., Ph.D.
721 N. Fielder Rd., Suite B
Arlington, TX 76012
(817) 460-5831

Testing, assessment, and career planning for high school seniors up to adults. Experience with learning disabilities.

*"In a typical test battery, inter-
est, personality, values, and abilities are measured to develop
recommendations."*

DALLAS

Douglas Bellamy, Ph.D.
12900 Preston Rd.
Dallas, TX 75230
(214) 404-8888
Testing, skill/interest assessment.

*"We explore the psychological as-
pects of career choices in depth."*

Career Action Associates
12655 N. Central Expwy.,
  Suite 512
Dallas, TX 75243
Metro (214) 269-5106 or
  (214) 392-7337
Rebecca Hayes, M.A., counseling; LPC, certified rehabilitation counselor

*Networking, workshops, career
and life planning, resume assistance, interviewing techniques,
resource library. Also works with
disabled and students.*

*"We help people become em-
ployed doing what they do best
and most enjoy doing."*

Career Dimensions
11520 N. Central Expwy.,
  Suite 141
Dallas, TX 75243
(214) 349-0573
Taunee Besson, B.A., business
  administration; CCC

*Networking, resume assistance,
interviewing techniques, salary
negotiation, goal setting, life
planning, relocation services.
Specializes in career/job-chang-
ing professionals and managers
and spouse relocations.*

*"I have twenty years of experi-
ence in corporate, social service,
and small business management.
I understand my clients because
I have 'walked in their
moccasins.' "*

Carol Duncan Enterprises Inc.
12900 Preston Rd., Suite 500
Dallas, TX 75230
(214) 385-1130
Carol Duncan, certified vocational evaluation specialist

*Career and life planning, resume
assistance, interviewing techniques, referrals, collection of job
resource books, directories, and
information on local employers.*

*"I am committed to creating a
custom-designed program for
each of my clients so that when
they are finished they have a
sense of purpose, a career goal,
life-style plan, and back-up
support."*

Lake Highlands Counseling
  Center
7475 Skillman St., Suite 101A
Dallas, TX 75231
(214) 348-4536
Marshall Metze, Ph.D.,
  psychology

*Testing, assessment, career and
life planning, resume assistance
and production, interviewing
techniques, referrals, resource
library.*

*"Practical applications of psy-
chology to business needs."*

Rehabilitation Services Associates Inc.
4607 Fairmount St.
Dallas, TX 75219
(214) 638-2586
Robert E. Boudreaux, M.Ed.,
  LPC

*Career and life planning, resume
assistance, job listings, interviewing techniques, referrals, resource library.*

*"We focus on past work history,
education, and counseling, and
pull this together for each individual to point them in the right
direction in the labor market."*

FORT WORTH

Career Clinic
1152 Country Club La.
Fort Worth, TX 76112
Metro (817) 654-9600
Richard S. Citrin, Ph.D.
Ann Teague, M.A., LPC

Support groups, networking, career and life planning, workshops, resume assistance, interviewing techniques, resource library.

"All populations served—teens through older clients, mid-life changes, and displaced homemakers."

Margaret S. Thompson, M.A., LPC
3813 Crestwood Terr.
Fort Worth, TX 76107
(817) 626-7023

Career/vocational testing and counseling for high school students, college students, and adults.

"My twenty-two years of experience as a counseling psychologist at Texas Christian University has provided a strong base of skills for working with high school and college students in choosing a college major and career direction."

GARLAND

Career Design Associates
2818 Country Club Rd.
Garland, TX 75043
(214) 278-4701
Helen Harkness, Ph.D., higher education and adult development

Support groups and networking, career and life planning, workshops, resume assistance, job listings, interviewing techniques, referrals, resource library.

"We provide a comprehensive service that will take the client through the entire career change and redirection ordeal."

IRVING

Career Management Resources
Towers at Williams Square
5215 N. O'Connor Rd.,
  Suite 200
Irving, TX 75039
(214) 556-0786
Mary Holdcroft, M.Ed.

Networking, job strategy planning, resume assistance and production, interviewing techniques and videotaped rehearsal, salary negotiation, resource library.

"Comprehensive career counseling and career management with special emphasis on spouse relocation career assistance."

Corporate Dynamics
Towers at Williams Square
5215 N. O'Connor Rd.,
  Suite 200
Irving, TX 75039
(214) 869-2470
Richard Poth, M.S., counseling
Linda Davidson, M.S., guidance and counseling, M.B.A.

Support groups and networking, career and life planning, workshops, resume assistance, interviewing techniques, job listings, referrals, books and directories.

"We are skillful, caring counselors who work with people in career transition, and we are consultants to corporations to manage organizational change."

PLANO

Career Consultations
520 Central Pkwy., Suite 107
Plano, TX 75074
(214) 578-1859
Ruth Glover, M.A., counseling

Support groups and networking, life planning, workshops, resume assistance, job listings, interviewing techniques, referrals, resource library. Specializes in spouse employment.

"We offer quality services at reasonable fees."

137

Career Focus Associates
2700 W. 15th St., Suite 312
Plano, TX 75075
(214) 596-1233
Jakie Statman, B.S., psychology

*Career planning, workshops, re-
sume assistance, interviewing
techniques, referrals, resource
library.*

*"I offer the most thorough and
comprehensive career assessment
with strong emphasis on both
skills and personal factors."*

RICHARDSON

Creative Career Counseling
703 Shadywood La.
Richardson, TX 75080
(214) 235-4689
Joan Youngblood, B.S., nursing

*Career and life planning, resume
assistance, interviewing techniques, resource library.*

*"Customized counseling process
designed for career changes,
work reality-shocked graduates,
reentry homemakers, employed
career fathers, and outplaced job
searchers."*

Professional Psychological
  Services
670 W. Arapaho Rd., Suite 3
Richardson, TX 75080
(214) 669-1266
Tim F. Branaman, Ph.D.

*Testing, skill/interest assessment,
career and life planning, resume
assistance, job-hunting books
and directories.*

*"Testing and counseling, usually
three to four sessions with a licensed psychologist."*

CAREER EXPLORATION AND TRAINING OPPORTUNITIES

Through volunteer work you can pick up organizational skills, financial management understanding, develop an improved ability to work with people, and become familiar with goal setting and long-range planning. The list is very long. A lot of the volunteer skills you learn are basic management skills."

> Patti Clapp, director of leadership development,
> Dallas Chamber of Commerce,
> and a longtime volunteer

So often job hunters just starting out hear the familiar refrain: "Sorry you don't have enough experience." Or workers find themselves in a job or field they don't like, faced with the prospect of changing positions or careers.

How can you get the experience and training so critical in today's competitive job market and at the same time explore what careers and types of jobs suit your interests, personality, and aptitudes?

The answer may be volunteer work, internships, apprenticeships, or leadership training. All offer innovative ways to obtain experience and training, develop and refine skills, expand your network, and work with a variety of people.

As a volunteer, you can gain training and experience, make valuable community contacts, and polish human relations skills. In an internship, you can receive education and work experience in your chosen field, usually while you're still in college or a new graduate. In an apprenticeship, you receive extensive on-the-job training in a specific field while earning a paycheck. Leadership training programs can help you develop your leadership potential and network while at the same time involving you in your community.

Many fields are embracing these work-learn programs as a low-risk, low-cost way to train new employees. Internships and volunteer work often lead to full-time positions at the company or organization that sponsored them. Interns and volunteers also often have more flexibility than permanent employees and can work in various departments or try different kinds of jobs.

If you're in school, ask your department head or career counseling office about internship, volunteer, or apprenticeship programs. If you're new to the area or changing careers, professional and community service organizations are good sources of information about local internship or volunteer programs.

VOLUNTEER WORK

The Dallas–Fort Worth area is full of examples of men and women who started out as volunteers and parlayed that experience into positions such as directors of social service agencies and foundations, social workers, and public relations managers.

Though not as fast as many volunteers would like, companies are also beginning to recognize the value of volunteer experience, and volunteers have found good positions in the private sector.

One of the best ways to get practical, useful experience as a volunteer is to serve on a board. Several organizations focus on training and recruiting people recommended because of their professional expertise to sit on boards of nonprofit groups, arts organizations, and community service agencies. Board members usually participate in hiring decisions, approve budgets, set goals, and provide leadership. In other words, they have management responsibilities. The difference is they don't get paid for this work as they would in a private enterprise.

If you think you would like to volunteer at a local organization, one of the following groups should be able to guide you.

Center for Non-Profit Management Inc.
2900 Live Oak St.
Dallas, TX 75204
(214) 826-3470

Management training and experience for nonprofit organizations. Aimed at administrators of nonprofit organizations.

Community Board Institute
Junior League of Dallas
8003 Inwood Rd.
Dallas, TX 75209
(214) 357-8822

Joint program of Junior League of Dallas and National Council of Jewish Women. Sponsors annual training seminar on skills needed to serve on the board of a nonprofit organization, arts group, or social services agency.

Retired Senior Volunteer
    Program
United Way of Metropolitan
    Tarrant County
210 E. 9th St.
Fort Worth, TX 76102
(817) 878-0122

Individualized volunteer job counseling to senior citizens.

Volunteer Center of Dallas
2816 Swiss Ave.
Dallas, TX 75204
(214) 744-1194

Dallas area clearinghouse for volunteer organizations. Consults with agencies and organizations for volunteer program development, matches volunteers to needs, trains managers of volunteer services.

Volunteer Center, Tarrant
    County
United Way of Metropolitan
    Tarrant County
210 E. 9th St.
Fort Worth, TX 76102
(817) 878-0099

Tarrant County clearinghouse for volunteer organizations. Consults with agencies and organizations for volunteer program development, matches volunteers to agency needs, trains managers of volunteer services. Offices in northeast and west Fort Worth and in Arlington.

INTERNSHIPS

"An internship is the answer to the age-old question of how you get experience. It's low risk for the interns, it's low risk for us. Either you find out you like the business or you find out you don't."
                    Greg Bustin, general manager,
                    Tracy-Locke Pharr Public Relations

Internships can be paid or unpaid. Either way, they offer a structured work experience with supervision and evaluation, usually for a specific period of time such as a summer or a semester.

Some fields, such as journalism and advertising, seldom hire new college graduates who haven't received experience through an internship. Other professions, including accounting, public relations, and engineering, also regularly offer internships. In Texas, architects must complete a comprehensive intern-architect development program, or IDP, to receive their board license.

The scope of internships varies from employer to employer. Some give interns immediate responsibility for particular projects. A local public relations firm, for example, makes sure its interns get exposed to a number of different areas: video production, staff meetings, research projects, and other areas of the agency's work. Other firms may give interns a less active role. Before you accept an internship, make sure you know what your responsibilities will be, what kind of experience you will gain, and whether or not you will be paid.

Internships usually are offered through a college or university, a particular company with a formal program, or a professional organization. The following listing includes some of the organizations with established internship programs. To find out whether there are any internships available in a particular field not listed here, contact the career counseling department of one of the community colleges or universities.

American Institute of Architects
Dallas Chapter
2811 McKinley Ave.
Dallas, TX 75204
(214) 871-2788

Forth Worth Chapter
4388 W. Vickery Blvd.,
  Suite 101
Fort Worth, TX 76107
(817) 763-0242
National AIA office jointly administers intern-architect development program. Area chapters can assign advisors to interns.

The Dallas Morning News
Communications Center
508 Young St.
Dallas, TX 75202
(214) 977-8222

Dallas's leading daily newspaper. Hires interns in news, general advertising, retail advertising, and classified advertising departments.

Ernst & Young
2001 Ross Ave., Suite 2800
Dallas, TX 75201
(214) 979-1700
Major accounting firm. Hires mainly summer interns.

Tracy-Locke Inc.
200 Crescent Ct., Suite 900
Dallas, TX 75250
(214) 969-9000
Major advertising and public relations firm. Hires interns throughout the year in advertising and public relations.

APPRENTICESHIPS

Apprenticeships use a combination of on-the-job training and instruction to teach their trade or craft and give working experience.

Apprentices work under the close supervision of workers at the journey level and usually are paid based on a percentage of the journey worker's wages—usually 35 to 40 percent in the Dallas–Fort Worth area. Some apprentice programs last up to four years. You don't have to be starting out to apply for an apprenticeship. Many organizations will take on entry-level apprentices as well as people with experience.

Most apprenticeship programs are sponsored jointly by employers and labor unions and focus on trades such as carpentry, bricklaying, or metalworking. Some apprenticeships are available in areas such as retail or computer operations, but the sponsors don't often recruit from the general public.

Apprenticeships must adhere to strict standards. The U.S. Department of Labor's Bureau of Apprenticeship and Training monitors apprenticeship programs, works with employers to identify their training needs, and advises them throughout the program. The bureau also issues certificates to apprentices upon completion of a registered program.

Local bureau offices are a good source of information about how an apprenticeship works. They can also offer suggestions or sources of information about apprenticeships in a particular field.

U.S. Department of Labor
Bureau of Apprenticeship and
   Training
525 Griffin St.
Dallas, TX 75202
(214) 767-4993

Fort Worth office:
819 Taylor St.
Fort Worth, TX 76102
(817) 334-3486

LEADERSHIP TRAINING

If you want to develop your leadership potential in the community as well as in the workplace, one of the area's many leadership training programs can help you.

These programs usually are sponsored or cosponsored by area Chambers of Commerce. Most are also affiliated with the National Association of Community Leadership Organizations. Here's the way they work: anyone may apply or nominate someone to participate in a leadership program. An admissions committee then selects a certain number of people based on their leadership potential. The leadership class meets periodically to examine issues in the community, develop leadership skills, and explore areas in which they can contribute to the community.

While not aimed at job and career, the skills acquired in such a program certainly translate to the workplace. You'll learn to work with a variety of people, explore how your community works and who the players are, and expand your contacts.

The alumni groups of area leadership programs read like a Who's Who of established business and community leaders as well as up-and-comers. Leadership alumni groups continue to be active in community affairs and are a premier networking group since their members represent so many industries and backgrounds.

Some of the area's programs are listed below but similar programs are available in cities throughout the area. Check with your local Chamber of Commerce.

The Dallas Alliance
Leadership and Organizational
  Skills Institute
1507 Pacific Ave., 3rd Floor
Dallas, TX 75201
(214) 948-3012
Sponsors workshops on negotiating, setting goals, resolving conflict, and building coalitions.

Leadership Dallas
Dallas Chamber of Commerce
1201 Elm St., Suite 2000
Dallas, TX 75270
(214) 746-6725
Contact: Patti Clapp
Nine-month program examining community-interest issues and developing leadership skills and volunteer careers. Maintains a data base of participants interested in becoming volunteers.

Leadership Fort Worth
P.O. Box 76101
Fort Worth, TX 76101
(817) 336-6364
Contact: Tiny Batts
Nine-month program examining community issues. Alumni group matches members who want to serve on nonprofit and community boards with organizations.

Women's Center of Dallas
3505 Turtle Creek Blvd.,
  Suite 103
Dallas, TX 75219
(214) 521-9606
In cooperation with the University of Texas at Dallas, holds annual one-day Women in Leadership Conference that encourages women to become community and corporate leaders.

144

AGENCIES

The difference between an employment agency and an executive search firm on retainer is time. An agency can't invest a great deal of time. They get your resume and send it out. You basically have a brokerage relationship in an employment agency. With an executive search firm, you have a consultative relationship. We invest a good amount of time at the front end understanding the company and the position."

Nat Turner, president, Paul & Turner Inc.

General employment agencies, executive search firms, and temporary employment agencies offer yet another option for the job hunter—if you're willing to give up some of your own job search independence and trust a third party to locate prospects for you. These employment professionals often have the inside track on jobs in a particular industry, may know in advance about positions becoming available, and can save you research time in identifying possible employers.

Sorting through the list of such services can be confusing, however. Companies vary widely in size, areas of specialization, and their degree of professionalism, so do your homework before you agree to use their services. The most important thing is to find out in advance who pays the fees for the jobs available. Also ask what other services the agency provides—help developing a job search strategy, for example, or preparing for interviews or training.

The best references, of course, are an agency's or executive search firm's reputation and a recommendation by someone you know who has used its services. You should also ask the

145

agency or firm about its history, track record, and specialties. If you have any doubts, consult the Better Business Bureau to see if others have experienced problems.

Many agencies specialize in specific industries. Such specialists are a good choice if you are interested in a particular industry. They know the business, what kinds of jobs are available, and have established relationships with key industry employers. They often get the first word about some of the best positions.

The selective listings that follow represent the kinds of professional employment services available throughout the Dallas–Fort Worth area Inclusion does not imply endorsement. Agencies and executive search firms in the listing were chosen based on their specialties and geographic locations.

EMPLOYMENT AGENCIES

Employment agencies act as the "go-betweens," matchmakers between companies trying to fill positions and job hunters seeking them. They receive a fee if one of their applicants is hired, usually paid by the company. Sometimes the job candidate pays, generally a percentage of the job's annual salary. The advice bears repeating: find out who pays before you sign anything or even fill out an application.

Agencies are an especially good resource for job hunters relocating to the area. Quality agencies have the experience and knowledge to save you time in researching the job market. There are, however, limitations to using an agency. The majority of their jobs are office and entry-level, although some agencies also handle lower-level professional and management positions. Most agency positions are for jobs with an annual salary under $50,000.

Among the agencies that specialize in particular occupational fields, accounting data processing, and law are three of the hottest specialties. The following is a selective listing of Dallas–Fort Worth agencies and their areas of specialization.

Accountants on Call
2001 Ross Ave., Suite 360
Dallas, TX 75201
(214) 979-9001
Temporary and permanent placement in accounting, bookkeeping, finance, data entry, and

support positions. Also north Dallas office.

Adia Personnel Services
600 N. Pearl St.
Dallas, TX 75201
(214) 953-1430

Permanent and temporary positions in administrative, advertising, data processing and word processing, communications, legal, insurance, accounting, field support. Offices throughout the area.

Attorney Resource
700 N. Pearl St., Suite 1720
Dallas, TX 75201
(214) 922-8050
Legal support personnel.

Aware Affiliates Personnel Service
901 Summit Ave.
Fort Worth, TX 76102
(817) 870-2590
Data processing, technical, and mortgage.

Carrollton Employment Service, Inc.
1925 Belt Line Rd., Suite 409
Carrollton, TX 75006
(214) 242-2176
Permanent and temporary positions. Specializes in administrative support.

DataPro Personnel Consultants
2001 One Galleria Tower
13355 Noel Rd.
Dallas, TX 75240
(214) 661-8600

Data processing, computer professionals.

Robert Half Inc.
Three NorthPark East, Suite 200
Dallas, TX 75231
(214) 363-3300

Fort Worth office:
1300 Summit Ave., Suite 228
Fort Worth, TX 76102
(817) 870-1200
Accounting, financial, and data processing.

Opportunity Unlimited Inc.
1244 Southridge Ct.
Fort Worth, TX 76053
(817) 280-9734
Engineering, computer sciences, electronics, and aerospace.

Snelling and Snelling
4975 Preston Park Blvd., Suite 160
Plano, TX 75093
(214) 985-1746
Billed as the world's largest employment service, with offices throughout the area. Specializes in administrative, sales, office services, and technical positions.

EXECUTIVE SEARCH FIRMS AND RECRUITERS

Executive search consultants—"headhunters" or "executive recruiters"—are employment professionals hired by a client company to find candidates for managerial, higher-level professional, and top management positions. Such firms operate on a contingency basis or on retainer, the latter meaning they get paid to search a particular position even if the company doesn't hire one of their candidates.

Companies usually pay executive search firms about 30 to 33 percent of the position's annual salary. The largest executive search firms in the Dallas–Fort Worth area search candidates for positions with annual salaries ranging from about $60,000 up to $150,000.

Generally, you won't get very far by calling area headhunters yourself or papering them with resumes. Some firms do add unsolicited resumes to their data bases, but normally executive search firms use their network of contacts and references to locate candidates. Unless your resume happens to land on a searcher's desk at exactly the time he or she is looking for someone with your exact qualifications, you probably won't get a response to an unsolicited inquiry.

The best advice for dealing with an executive search firm is to be prepared if you happen to meet a consultant at a professional meeting or if one calls you about a job. Find out about the searcher's background and the types of positions he or she generally handles. Try to ascertain if he or she really understands the job requirements and the company—and what happened to the predecessor in the position.

Remember that executive search consultants can be valuable contacts even if you're not interested in the job. Many firms also have management consultant practices and are extremely knowledgeable about the area job market and trends in specific industries. Establishing a relationship with a good consultant could get you into their data base of contacts and pay off in the future.

The following are some of the area's major executive search firms as well as those specializing in key industries.

Ernst & Young Executive
  Search
2001 Ross Ave., Suite 2800
Dallas, TX 75201
(214) 979-1700
Manufacturing, health care, financial services.

Heidrick & Struggles Inc.
1999 Bryan St., Suite 1919
Dallas, TX 75201
(214) 220-2130
Upper-middle- and upper-level executive positions.

Henard Associates
970 Rolm Tower
15303 Dallas Pkwy.
Dallas, TX 75248
(214) 991-7151
Consumer packaged goods, food and beverage, restaurants, electronics.

Korn/Ferry International
500 N. Akard St., Suite 3950
Dallas, TX 75201
(214) 954-1834
Education, energy, entertainment, fashion/retail, financial services, health care, high technology, hospitality/leisure, real estate.

Management Recruiters of
  Plano
101 E. Park Blvd., Suite 355
Plano, TX 75074
(214) 424-3339
Banking, construction, legal, data processing, telecommunications, transportation, manufacturing. Offices throughout the area.

Paul & Turner Inc.
12221 Merit Dr., Suite 1660
Dallas, TX 75251
(214) 386-9991

Computers, telecommunications, semiconductors, electronic publishing.

Paul R. Ray & Co. Inc.
301 Commerce St., Suite 2300
Fort Worth, TX 76102
(817) 334-0500
General management. Also Dallas office.

Spencer Stuart
1717 Main St., Suite 5300
Dallas, TX 75201
(214) 658-1777
High technology, energy, financial services.

Witt Associates Inc.
Three Lincoln Center
5430 LBJ Fwy., Suite 270
Dallas, TX 75240
(214) 770-2070
Health care.

TEMPORARY EMPLOYMENT AGENCIES

Temporary employment agencies can be one of your best alternatives if you need money and flexible hours while you're job hunting, want to "try out" different company environments or brush up on certain skills.

The "temp" business is intensely competitive in the Dallas–Fort Worth area and agencies have become more savvy about cultivating a pool of qualified temporary workers. Several temp agencies specialize in key area industries, such as data processing, electronics, law, or health care. Many temporary agencies offer their employees instruction on the latest computer, word processing, and software equipment. Some even offer paid vacations and benefits if you've worked a certain number of hours.

Normally, though, temp work pays much less than a permanent position. And while temp work gives you exposure to a variety of working environments, some people may find it hard to adjust to changing corporate cultures, department work styles, or schedules.

On the other hand, temp work can be a good way to get your foot in the door of a particular company or field. It can lead to permanent employment if a company has an opening and already knows you and your work. If you work for an agency that provides both temporary and permanent employment, though, be sure to find out if any fees are involved if your temporary job leads to a permanent one.

The following is a selective list of some area temporary employment agencies reflecting the variety of area specializations. Most agencies have multiple locations throughout the area, so you may want to ask about the office nearest you.

Accountemps
Three NorthPark East, Suite
  200
Dallas, TX 75231
(214) 363-3600

*Accounting, bookkeeping, bark-
ing, data entry, systems analysts,
programmers, word processing.
Owned by Robert Half Inc.*

Bank Temporaries Inc.
5323 Spring Valley Rd., Suite
  207
Dallas, TX 75240
(214) 243-8484

Financial services personnel.

CDI Corp.
8700 N. Stemmons Fwy., Suite
  112
Dallas, TX 75235
(214) 905-9075

*Technicians, electronic assembly,
telecommunications specialists,
quality control inspectors, engineers, programmers, designers-
drafters, computer-aided design
and manufacturing specialists.*

Favorite Nurses
800 W. Airport Fwy., Suite 526
Irving, TX 75062
Metro (214) 445-0677

*Supplemental staffing for nurses,
including RNs, LVNs, and aides.*

Kelly Temporary Services
Downtown office
500 N. Akard St., Suite 230
Dallas, TX 75271
(214) 740-3666

Downtown Fort Worth office:
801 Cherry St., Suite 2365
Fort Worth, TX 76102
(817) 332-7807

Nation's largest temporary

*agency with offices throughout
the area. Placements include
word processing, marketing, data
entry, clerical.*

Manpower Temporary Services
Downtown office
500 N. Akard St., Suite 2880
Dallas, TX 75202
(214) 954-0093

Downtown Fort Worth office:
777 Main St., Suite 1515
Fort Worth, TX 76102
(817) 877-1212

*Word processing, data entry op-
erators, secretarial. Offices
throughout the area.*

Norrell Temporaries
Downtown office
1201 Elm St., Suite 2677
Dallas, TX 75270
(214) 749-0472

Downtown Fort Worth office:
301 Commerce St., Suite 1310
Fort Worth, TX 76102
(817) 870-1999

*Clerical, word processing, mar-
keting/convention. Offices
throughout the area.*

Personnel Pool
One Summit Ave., Suite 101
Fort Worth, TX 76102
(817) 335-6333

*Clerical, bookkeeping, data entry,
word processing. An H&R Block
company. Other area offices.*

WordTemps
1700 Alma Rd., Suite 107
Plano, TX 75075
(214) 422-9844

*Word processing. Several offices
throughout the area.*

150

DALLAS– FORT WORTH AREA BUSINESS AND INDUSTRY

The only thing you need to find a job in Dallas–Fort Worth is desire. We're in an economy that has fundamentally changed. There is a tremendous requirement for manpower in virtually all categories of business, from small companies to large. I can't think of a better place in the country to look for a job or for companies that have jobs and are looking to fill them."

Rick Douglas, president, North Texas Commission

Whether you're corporate or artistic, like to work with numbers or work with your hands, starting a career or wanting to change the one you've got, the Dallas–Fort Worth area offers a wealth of employment possibilities.

Although oil and gas, banking, and real estate are still recovering from the severe economic pounding they took in the late 1980s and won't provide the level of jobs they did in the past, other industries such as high technology, telecommunications, transportation, and health care are growing and creating many of the new jobs in the area.

High-technology and telecommunications continue to attract new players, including a major influx by Japanese companies. The air transportation industry is in the midst of a huge expansion of facilities and services. And Dallas is on the way to positioning itself as an internationally recognized medical center.

Because of their central geographic location, Dallas and Fort Worth are also headquarters cities. The area is home base to Fortune 500 companies such as Texas Instruments,

American Airlines, LTV J. C. Penney, Exxon, and Kimberly-Clark. A wave of corporate relocations and expansions in recent years is expected to bring thousands more new jobs to the area in the 1990s.

In addition to large companies, Dallas–Fort Worth also offers opportunities in small business, nonprofit, and government. Many companies now respected in their fields were yesterday's start-ups—Dallas Semiconductor and Convex Computer, for example. In the employment lists that follow we have tried to include both major employers as well as smaller companies with the potential to grow and add jobs.

We've also tried to capture the flavor and the range of job possibilities within key industries. In your job search, keep an open mind and try not to confine yourself to only one industry listing. For example, if you're looking for a job in accounting, it would be logical to turn to the "Accounting" list. But remember that not only accounting firms need accountants, they're also needed by banks, insurance companies, manufacturers, high-technology firms, and others. Try to imagine what other industries might fit your education, training, experience, and interest.

Use the business and industry listings as a starting point to help with your own *self-directed* survey of companies and organizations in fields that interest you. Once you're ready to explore further, use the section "Libraries, Directories, and Publications" to research these companies and to lead you to other employers in a particular industry.

For some industries, we've cited professional organizations that can provide networking opportunities, job lines, or other services useful to job hunters. For more information about these resources, see under "Business Networks and Professional Associations."

We've deliberately avoided listing personnel office contacts for each company because those persons rarely make the hiring decisions. Once you've identified companies or organizations where you might want to work, use your network of contacts and other resources in the guide to find out who makes the hiring decisions for the job you're seeking. Contact them directly. You'll be way ahead of other job hunters whose resumes may have been lost or filed away in the personnel office.

ACCOUNTING

"Given the relocation of major companies down here, the Dallas/Fort Worth International Airport expansion, the ability to go nonstop from Dallas–Fort Worth to almost anywhere in the world—there's a whole range of reasons why the Metroplex is emerging as a major business center. Whether it's getting a tax return filed, reorganizing an accounting department, or installing a new computer system, the need for accounting services is unparalleled. And the opportunities for young people in the accounting profession have probably never been better."

Dennis J. Wander and James V. Ivy,
managing partners, Ernst & Young

Accounting appears to be headed for a period of growth, bringing with it a strong demand for skilled workers. The Texas Employment Commission calls accountants and auditors one of the twenty "hottest jobs" in Texas, projecting an annual demand for 4,550 new accountants and auditors through 1995.

Many of those job openings will be in the Dallas–Fort Worth area, the state's financial center. The largest accounting firms—known as the "Big Eight" before several of them decided to merge—all have offices in Dallas and most have offices in both cities. Hundreds of smaller firms are scattered throughout the area, although they also have a smaller number of job openings and their range of services may be more limited. In addition, all sorts of locally based companies need in-house accountants, auditors, and financial officers.

Specialization is the watchword in accounting today, especially in the largest firms. Accounting mirrors the market in which it operates, so area offices tend to specialize in financial institutions, aerospace, high technology, health care, real estate, the hospitality industry, and oil and gas.

The largest accounting firms employ anywhere from a hundred to more than a thousand people in their area offices. They hire most of their new employees directly out of college and then give them several years of training. But the number of students majoring in accounting is dwindling, and competition is fierce for accounting graduates with good grades, leadership qualities, and communication skills. The big firms have aggressive college recruiting programs to identify prospects, and many offer internship programs to get young people into the job pipeline.

If you already have expertise in a particular industry or business area, you may want to consider working as a consultant at an accounting firm. Management consulting is one of the fastest growing segments of the accounting profession. Consultants work with clients on everything from writing a business plan to installing a new computer system. The firms often have to look outside for talent for their consulting businesses. Computer systems consulting is a particularly hot area right now.

The local chapters of the Texas Society of Certified Public Accountants are good resources for job hunters in the accounting profession. The Dallas chapter keeps a resume file for its members. The Fort Worth chapter publishes a newsletter and sells space to anyone wanting to take out a classified ad. Both chapters also publish membership directories. Refer to the section "Business Networks and Professional Organizations" for more information about these groups.

The following is a list of the largest public accounting firms in the area, as well as some smaller, established firms and their primary services.

Arthur Andersen & Co.
901 Main St., Suite 5300
Dallas, TX 75265
(214) 741-8300

Fort Worth office:
801 Cherry St., Suite 1200
Fort Worth, TX 76102
(817) 870-3000

Financial consulting, tax, information systems, litigation support, computer integrated manufacturing.

Bland, Garvey & Taylor Inc.
1202 Richardson Dr., Suite 203
Richardson, TX 75080
(214) 231-2503

Accounting, audit, tax, consulting services for small businesses and professionals.

Coopers & Lybrand
1999 Bryan St., Suite 3000
Dallas, TX 75201
(214) 754-5000

Fort Worth office:
301 Commerce St., Suite 1900
Fort Worth, TX 76102
Metro (817) 429-2410 or
  (817) 332-2243

Auditing, tax, management consulting, litigation, business reorganization services, industry specialties.

Deloitte & Touche
1400 Lincoln Plaza
Dallas, TX 75201
(214) 954-4500

Fort Worth office:
801 Cherry St., Suite 2340
Fort Worth, TX 76102-6801
Metro (817) 654-2777 or
  (817) 336-2531

Audit, tax, emerging business services, consulting, industry specialties. Firm resulted from merger of Deloitte Haskins & Sells and Touche Ross & Co.

Ernst & Young
2001 Ross Ave., Suite 2800
Dallas, TX 75201
(214) 979-1700

Fort Worth office:
2200 Texas American Bank
  Bldg.
Fort Worth, TX 76102
(817) 335-2700

Accounting, audit, tax and financial planning, management con-

154

sulting, entrepreneurial services, industry specialties. Firm resulted from merger of Ernst & Whinney and Arthur Young & Co.

Grant Thornton
800 Allied Bank Tower
Dallas, TX 75202
(214) 855-7300

Audit, tax, management consulting, capital formation.

Lane, Gorman, Trubitt & Co.
1909 Woodall Rogers Fwy.,
    Suite 400
Dallas, TX 75201-2232
(214) 871-7500

Accounting, audit, tax, consulting services, financial planning.

Laventhol & Horwath
2121 San Jacinto St., Suite
    1700
Dallas, TX 75201
(214) 754-7100

Accounting, audit, tax, hospitality, real estate and leisure time consulting, entrepreneurial services.

Kenneth Leventhal & Co.
2001 Ross Ave., Suite 1600
Dallas, TX 75201
(214) 969-0900

Consulting, audit, tax.

Pannell Kerr Foster
14001 Dallas Pkwy., Suite 500
Dallas, TX 75240
(214) 661-1843

Accounting, audit, tax, hospitality and real estate consulting and appraisal, management advisory services.

Peat Marwick Main & Co.
1501 Elm St., Suite 400
Dallas, TX 75201
(214) 754-2000

Fort Worth office:
301 Commerce St., Suite 2500
Fort Worth, TX 76102
(817) 335-2655

Audit, tax, management consulting, industry specialties, litigation support.

Price Waterhouse
1700 Pacific Ave., Suite 1400
Dallas, TX 75201
(214) 922-8040

Litigation, tax, industry specialties, emerging business.

Weaver and Tidwell
1500 Commerce Bldg.
307 W. 7th St.
Fort Worth, TX 76102
(817) 332-7905

Dallas office:
Two Galleria Tower
13455 Noel Rd., Suite 520
Dallas, TX 75240
Metro (214) 263-3978 or
    (214) 490-1970

Accounting, audit, tax planning and compliance, management consulting, information systems.

ADVERTISING AND PUBLIC RELATIONS

"A lot of people who want to come into the advertising business from non-related fields like banking, restaurant management, and real estate just don't realize they don't have the technical skills. From the outside world advertising looks pretty simple—you sit around and think up ideas. But behind that scene is a tremendous amount of technical knowledge that you can't get in non-related fields."

Penny Plueckhahn, vice president and director of operations and human resources, Tracy-Locke Inc.

Dallas–Fort Worth isn't the New York or the Los Angeles of the advertising and public relations world, but it's still a major, competitive market with job opportunities. The key word is *experience*.

Because large agencies hold prestigious national as well as regional accounts, they usually require at least two to three years of experience. The smaller agencies are more flexible in hiring college graduates or career changers—*if* they've held internships or received some kind of complementary experience.

Young people who want to break into advertising should get some experience in college, perhaps through an internship, and also get two to three years of experience at a small shop or in a smaller market. On the other hand, most agencies don't care whether you have an advertising degree or not.

Ad agencies have openings in a variety of positions: account executives, media planners and buyers, traffic and coordination, production artists, typesetters, copywriters, audiovisual technicians, broadcast production, even talent contract negotiation. PR agencies, corporate communications departments, nonprofit organizations, and trade associations are looking for production art assistants, copywriters, circulation managers, communications managers, and others. Computer experience is a requirement for many of the jobs.

Several local organizations are good resources for the job hunter. These include the Public Relations Society of America, the International Association of Business Communicators, Women in Communications, and the Dallas Press Club. The PRSA and the IABC have set up a recorded job hot line (214-744-6056) that lists available openings. These organizations also sponsor meetings and special events and publish newsletters that offer good opportunities for networking and finding out more about the local industry. The local chapters of the PRSA periodically hold seminars that discuss the basics of PR. For more information on these organizations and their programs, consult the section "Business Networks and Professional Organizations."

The listing that follows represents some of Dallas–Fort Worth's largest agencies, as well as some smaller shops.

Anderson Fischel Thompson
5151 Belt Line Rd., Suite 700
Dallas, TX 75240
(214) 233-8461
Advertising/public relations.

The Bloom Cos. Inc.
7701 Stemmons Fwy.
Dallas, TX 75247-4214
(214) 638-8100
Advertising/public relations.

Bozell Inc.
201 E. Carpenter Fwy.
Irving, TX 75062
(214) 556-1100
Advertising/public relations.

Dally Advertising Inc.
1320 S. University Dr.,
  Suite 501
Fort Worth, TX 76107
(817) 332-5299
Advertising/public relations.

Hill & Knowlton Inc.
1500 One Dallas Centre
350 N. St. Paul St.
Dallas, TX 75201
(214) 979-0090
Public relations.

Keller-Crescent Co.
102 Decker Ct., Suite 100
Irving, TX 75062
(214) 541-0700
Advertising/public relations.

Krause & Young Inc.
501 Elm St., Suite 300
Dallas, TX 75202
(214) 741-7500
Advertising.

Larkin Meeder & Schweidel
  Inc.
7800 Stemmons Fwy., Suite 770
Dallas, TX 75247
(214) 688-7070
Advertising.

Levenson Levenson & Hill Inc.
5215 N. O'Connor Rd., Suite
  1100
Irving, TX 75039
Metro (214) 263-4145
Advertising/public relations.

McCann-Erickson Inc.
10330 N. Central Expwy., Suite
  246
Dallas, TX 75231
(214) 361-1135
Advertising.

McKone & Co.
1900 Westridge Dr.
Irving, TX 75038
Metro (214) 751-0523 or
  (214) 550-7433
Advertising/public relations.

Pavlik & Associates
100 E. 15th St., Suite 320
Fort Worth, TX 76102
(817) 429-0062
Advertising/public relations.

PR/Texas
6102 Grove St.
Fort Worth, TX 76102
(817) 332-6522
Public relations.

Puskar Gibbon Chapin Inc.
3500 Maple Ave., Suite 900
Dallas, TX 75219
(214) 528-5400
Advertising.

The Richards Group
10000 N. Central Exp'wy., Suite
  1200
Dallas, TX 75231
(214) 891-5700
Advertising/public relations.

Todd Co.
1301 S. Bowen Rd., Suite 260
Arlington, TX 76013
(817) 461-8633
Marketing communications.

Tracy-Locke Inc.
200 Crescent Ct., Suite 900
Dallas, TX 75250
(214) 969-9000
Advertising/public relations.

Young & Rubicam–Dallas Inc.
2695 Villa Creek Dr., Suite 120
Dallas, TX 75234
(214) 620-9870
Advertising.

Witherspoon
1000 W. Weatherford St.
Fort Worth, TX 76102
Metro (817) 429-1541
Advertising/public relations.

AEROSPACE AND DEFENSE

The Dallas–Fort Worth area is one of the nation's top centers for aerospace and defense research, development, and manufacturing. About one hundred thousand area residents work on such high-profile projects as the B-2 Stealth bomber, F-16 fighter, V-22 tilt-rotor, and the space shuttle, and on top-secret programs.

Some of the largest contractors—General Dynamics, LTV, and Bell Helicopter Textron—build aircraft and aircraft parts. Clustered around them are hundreds of components and spare parts manufacturers, machine shops, and other small businesses.

What makes the area industry unique, though, is the proliferation of defense electronics companies, particularly radar, intelligence, and electronic warfare developers. Some make the sophisticated systems that aircraft, tanks, and ships need to navigate, communicate, plan missions, and spy on adversaries. Others develop the electronics that control missiles and other weapons and computerized simulation systems for training.

Aerospace companies hire engineers who design products and develop processes and technologies, as well as production workers. These people often are hired directly out of college or trade schools for entry-level positions. Most companies prefer to "grow their own" core of workers and promote from within. Hiring from other aerospace companies is more common in mid- to upper-level positions.

While the defense industry is a major source of area employment, it is notoriously cyclical. After booming in the early to mid-1980s, the industry will be in a period of flat or even negative growth for the next several years. Expected cutbacks in defense spending could affect employment in this sector, particularly for companies that make "big-ticket" items like aircraft. Some contractors have already tightened their belts and laid off hundreds of workers.

According to industry officials and economists, however, many defense electronics companies will thrive even in a tight budget environment because their products will be in greater demand to upgrade existing aircraft, tanks, and ships.

The following is a sampling of the area's variety of aerospace and defense firms.

Aerospatiale Helicopter Corp.
2701 Forum Dr.
Grand Prairie, TX 75053-4005
(214) 641-0000
Military and commercial helicopters.

BEI Defense Systems Co. Inc.
11312 S. Pipeline Rd.
Euless, TX 76039
(817) 267-8191
Rocket systems.

Bell Helicopter Textron Inc.
600 E. Hurst Blvd.
Hurst, TX 76053
(817) 280-2011
Military and commercial helicopters, including the V-22 tilt-rotor.

Boeing Aerospace and Electronics–Corinth
7801 S. Stemmons Fwy.
Corinth, TX 75065
(817) 497-7600
Electronic components and subsystems.

Electrospace Systems Inc.
1301 E. Collins Blvd.
Richardson, TX 75081
(214) 470-2000
Installs telecommunications and navigation systems and modifies aircraft.

E-Systems Inc.
6250 LBJ Fwy.
Dallas, 75240
(214) 661-1000
Intelligence, reconnaissance, electronic warfare, command, control, and communications systems. Modifies and maintains aircraft, including the President's Air Force One.

General Dynamics Corp.
Fort Worth Division
North Grants La.
Fort Worth, TX 76108
(817) 777-2000
Military aircraft, including the F-16.

Hughes Simulation Systems Inc.
Arlington Division
2200 Arlington Downs Rd.
Arlington, TX 76011
(817) 640-5000
Flight simulators, trainers, computer-based training.

Hydroscience Inc.
2659 Nova Dr.
Dallas, TX 75229
(214) 247-9052
U.S. Navy sonar and surveillance equipment.

Intercontinental Manufacturing Co.
1200 N. Glenbrook Dr.
Garland, TX 75040
(214) 276-5131
Bomb bodies, precision aluminum forgings, missile hardware, air frames.

Menasco Aerosystems
4000 Hwy. 157
Euless, TX 76039
(817) 283-4471
Military and commercial landing gear.

LTV Corp.
Aircraft Products Group
9314 W. Jefferson Blvd.
Dallas, TX 75211
(214) 266-2011
Airframe structures.

LTV Corp.
Missiles and Electronics Group
1902 W. Fwy.
Grand Prairie, TX 75051
(214) 266-2011
*Multiple-launch rocket system,
tactical missile systems, defense
electronics systems.*

Merit Technology Inc.
5068 W. Plano Pkwy.
Plano, TX 75093
(214) 248-2502
*Software and expert systems for
mission planning and
simulation.*

Optic-Electronic Corp.
11545 Pagemill Rd.
P.O. Box 740668
Dallas, TX 75243
(214) 349-0190
*Laser range finders, target desig-
nators, night vision equipment,
and other optic systems.*

Rockwell International Corp.
Collins Defense
    Communications
3200 E. Renner Rd.
Richardson, TX 75081
(214) 705-0000
*Command, control, communica-
tion, and intelligence systems,
telecommunications systems, aircraft modification services.*

Technology Development Corp.
621 Six Flags Dr.
Arlington, TX 76011
(817) 640-7274
*Computer software for automatic
test equipment.*

Texas Instruments Inc.
Defense Systems and Electron-
    ics Group
8505 Forest La.
P.O. Box 660246
Dallas, TX 75266
(214) 995-2011
*Missiles and missile guidance
systems, airborne radars, electro-
optic systems.*

UTL Corp.
1508 W. Mockingbird La.
Dallas, TX 75235
(214) 638-6688
Electronic warfare systems.

Varo Inc.
2203 W. Walnut St.
P.O. Box 461426
Garland, TX 75046-1426
(214) 487-4100
*Night vision systems, power sup-
plies, missile launchers.*

APPAREL

The Dallas–Fort Worth area has long been famous for its
garment-manufacturing industry. The presence of the Apparel Mart and the Menswear Mart, part of the nation's largest inland market center complex, have also made the area
one of the nation's top apparel wholesaling hubs.

The Apparel Mart ranks second only to the New York mart
in dollar volume of wholesale goods sold each year. Retailers
come to the mart to purchase their goods from a variety of
manufacturers represented in showrooms rather than visit
each one individually at different geographic locations.

Because of the presence of the marts, many apparel manufacturers have located a few miles northwest of downtown
Dallas. The area's industry includes a number of small, in-

novative designers like Cristina and Jan Barboglio, as well as nationally known manufacturers and designers like Haggar, Prophecy, and Victor Costa. Western boots, hats, and clothing are an area specialty, with many of these manufacturers located in Fort Worth.

The local apparel business has been hurt by rising costs that are forcing some manufacturers to move their operations overseas. The slump in the local economy in recent years has also forced several large regional retailers to consolidate, resulting in fewer customers for apparel manufacturers' products. As a result, job opportunities vary from company to company, depending on their lines and the markets they serve.

Jobs in the apparel industry run the gamut from the actual point of design to the modeling and distribution of the finished product. They include designers, patternmakers, stylists, production assistants, sample makers, fitting advisors, fabric buyers, manufacturers' representatives, sales representatives, and models.

The listing that follows includes some of the area's designers, manufacturers, and companies that service the apparel industry. Retailers are listed separately under "Retailing and Wholesale Merchandising."

Barboglio
4949 Beeman Ave.
Dallas, TX 75223
(214) 824-3600
Designer of women's sportswear and dresses.

Byn-Mar
2952 Ladybird La.
Dallas, TX 75220
(214) 350-7011
Manufacturer of women's clothing.

Computerized Apparel Production Services Inc.
4949 Beeman Ave.
Dallas, TX 75223
(214) 826-7500
Computerized grading, marking, and patternmaking services.

Victor Costa Inc.
7600 Ambassador Row
Dallas, TX 75247
(214) 634-1133
Women's clothing designer.

Dallas Market Center Co.
2300 N. Stemmons Fwy.
Dallas, TX 75258
(214) 637-2171
Operator of Apparel Mart and Menswear Mart.

Kim Dawson Agency
2300 N. Stemmons Fwy.
Dallas, TX 75207
(214) 638-2414
The area's premier talent and modeling agency.

Haggar Apparel Co.
6113 Lemmon Ave.
Dallas, TX 75209
(214) 352-8481
Corporate headquarters for sportswear manufacturer.

Ginnie Johansen Designs
1365 Regal Row
Dallas, TX 75231
(214) 631-1180
Accessories designer and manufacturer.

Justin Industries Inc.
2821 W. 7th St.
Fort Worth, TX 76107
(817) 336-5125
Makes Justin and Nocona brand boots.

Malouf Co. Inc.
944 S. Lamar St.
Dallas, TX 75202
(214) 565-0126
Manufacturer of women's clothing.

Microdynamics Inc.
10461 Brockwood Rd.
Dallas, TX 75238
(214) 343-1170
Develops computer-aided design systems for footwear and apparel industries.

Prophecy Corp.
1302 Champion Circle
Carrollton, TX 75011
(214) 247-1900
Women's sportswear manufacturer.

Resistol Hats
601 Marion Dr.
Garland, TX 75042
(214) 494-0511
Manufacturer of cowboy hats and headwear. Known worldwide for its fine cowboy hats.

Westmoor Manufacturing
4901 N. Fwy.
Fort Worth, TX 76106
(817) 625-2841
Western clothing manufacturer.

Williamson-Dickie Manufacturing Co.
319 Lipscomb St.
Fort Worth, TX 76104
(817) 336-7201
Manufacturer best known for its Dickies label work clothes.

ARCHITECTURE AND INTERIOR DESIGN

The skylines of Dallas and Fort Worth changed dramatically in the early 1980s as boldly designed, ultramodern office buildings, apartments, and condominiums seemed to sprout all over the area almost overnight. The real estate boom, though, created a severe overdevelopment situation. Fewer buildings were constructed in the late 1980s, and many architectural firms saw their business decline. Some architects even left the area to follow building booms in other parts of the country.

Though most area firms have less business than they had before, the projects they do have are less speculative. Veteran architects who have weathered their profession's cycles before say they are confident business will pick up again, though probably not at the breakneck pace of the last decade. Despite a wave of corporate relocations and expansions, new municipal projects, and renovations of existing buildings, competition for new business is tough.

The good news is that local firms are hiring architects and

interior designers. Most of the larger firms look for people with one to six years of experience, but many also hire talented new graduates of architectural schools for entry-level positions.

The Dallas chapter of the American Insitute of Architects maintains a job book containing classified ads of firms looking for individuals. The Dallas and Fort Worth chapters also maintain a resume file for members. For more information on these organizations, see under "Business Networks and Professional Organizations."

Since many firms handle both architectural and engineering consulting, also check the listing under "Engineering" for additional employers.

Below are some of the area's architectural firms, including very large firms that employ hundreds of architects as well as smaller organizations.

Bernard Johnson Taylor
  Hewlett
2081 Hutton Dr., Suite 119
Carrollton, TX 75006
(214) 620-9262

Corgan Associates Architects
501 Elm St., Suite 500
Dallas, TX 75202
(214) 748-2000

Cunningham Architects
2700 Fairmount St., Suite 200
Dallas, TX 75201
(214) 855-5272

Good Fulton & Farrell
  Architects
2201 Ross Ave., Suite 300
Dallas, TX 75201
(214) 979-0028

Graham Associates Inc.
616 Six Flags Dr., Suite 400
Arlington, TX 76011
(817) 640-8535

HDR Inc.
12700 Hillcrest Rd., Suite 125
Dallas, TX 75230
(214) 960-4000
Dallas office of Omaha, Nebraska, firm.

Hellmuth, Obata & Kassabaum
  Inc.
6688 N. Central Expwy., Suite
  700
Dallas, TX 75206
(214) 739-6688
Dallas office of St. Louis firm.

HKS Inc.
700 N. Pearl St.
1111 Plaza of the Americas
Dallas, TX 75201
(214) 969-5599
Dallas's largest firm.

JPJ Architects Inc.
5910 N. Central Expwy., Suite
  1200
Dallas, TX 75206
(214) 987-8000

Albert S. Komatsu & Associates
  Inc.
550 Bailey Ave., Suite 715
Fort Worth, TX 76107
(817) 332-1914

Parker/Croston Partnership Inc.
3311 Hamilton Ave.
Fort Worth, TX 76147
Metro (817) 429-0320 or
  (817) 332-8464

RTKL Associates Inc.
2828 Routh St., Suite 200
Dallas, TX 75201
(214) 871-8877
Dallas office of Baltimore firm.

SHWC Inc.
5601 MacArthur Blvd.
Irving, TX 75038
(214) 550-0700

Womack-Humphreys Architects
  Inc.
5430 LBJ Fwy., Suite 1000
Dallas, TX 75240
(214) 770-2300

THE ARTS

Dallas–Fort Worth prides itself on being the state's cultural center. The area is home to internationally known art museums, as well as theaters, art galleries, ballet, opera, and symphony orchestras.

Fort Worth's Kimbell Art Museum, featuring works from the beginning of civilization to the early twentieth century, has been called the finest art museum of its size in the United States. Fort Worth is also home to several Western art museums showcasing works by Georgia O'Keeffe, Charles M. Russell, and Frederic Remington.

The Kimbell is in the process of doubling its exhibition space, the Dallas Museum of Art in the downtown Arts District is expanding its permanent collection, and the Dallas Symphony Orchestra has a new hall. Both cities have many art galleries and theaters catering to tastes ranging from the traditional to the avant garde.

Dallas is one of a few Texas cities to have a major resident theater with an acting company—the Dallas Theater Center. At the other end of the spectrum, the Deep Ellum area east of downtown Dallas has several small theaters that stage original and off-Broadway productions. Several smaller cities in the area also have community theaters.

The weak economy, however, has taken its toll on the arts. The Dallas Ballet Association ceased dance productions because of a lack of funds. Funding is tight for all arts organizations, which rely more than ever on volunteers to work behind the scenes. There are still paid jobs available for actors, artistic and managing directors, set designers, and musicians, but they are scarce. Some theaters have union contracts with actors; others pay actors a nominal fee or pay them "when possible."

The biggest job opportunities appear to be in such service-related arts positions as art consultants, appraisers, and teachers. Jobs are also available in fund-raising and community and public relations. Also keep in mind that a few large corporations may hire in-house art consultants to buy art for corporate investment. These jobs require very special qualifications and are hard to get. Volunteering for an arts organization offers good experience if you're interested in working in the arts but can't find a permanent position.

ART

Amon Carter Museum
3501 Camp Bowie Blvd.
Fort Worth, TX 76107
(817) 738-1933
Western art museum.

Dallas Museum of Art
1717 N. Harwood St.
Dallas, TX 75201
(214) 922-1200
Fine arts museum.

Gerald Peters Gallery
2913 Fairmount St.
Dallas, TX 75201
(214) 969-9410
Fine arts gallery.

Kimbell Art Museum
3333 Camp Bowie Blvd.
Fort Worth, TX 76107
(817) 332-8451
Fine arts museum.

Modern Art Museum of Fort
  Worth
1309 Montgomery St.
Fort Worth, TX 76107
(817) 738-9215
Modern art museum.

Sid Richardson Collection of
  Western Art
309 Main St.
Fort Worth, TX 76102
(817) 332-6554
Western art collection.

DANCE

Ballet Dallas
309 S. Pearl Expwy.
Dallas, TX 75201
(214) 748-3930

Dallas Black Dance Theatre
2627 Flora St.
Dallas, TX 75221
(214) 871-2376

Fort Worth Ballet
6845 Green Oaks Rd.
Fort Worth, TX 76116
(817) 763-0207

MUSIC

The Dallas Opera
1925 Elm St., Suite 400
Dallas, TX 75201
(214) 979-0123

Dallas Symphony Orchestra
2301 Flora St., Suite 300
Dallas, TX 75201
(214) 954-1700

Fort Worth Opera Association
3505 W. Lancaster Ave.
Fort Worth, TX 76107
(817) 731-0833

Fort Worth Symphony
  Orchestra
4401 Trail Lake Dr.
Fort Worth, TX 76109
(817) 921-2676

Richardson Symphony
  Orchestra
2480 Promenade Center
Richardson, TX 75080
(214) 234-4195

THEATER

Addison Centre Theatre
15600 Julian St.
Addison, TX 75001
(214) 934-3913
Community theater.

Casa Mañana Musicals Inc.
3101 W. Lancaster Ave.
Fort Worth, TX 76107
(817) 332-9319
Musicals.

Dallas Alliance Theatre
2204 Commerce St.
Dallas, TX 75201
(214) 748-7667
Community theater.

Dallas Theater Center
3636 Turtle Creek Blvd.
Dallas, TX 75219-5598
(214) 526-8857
Dallas's oldest legitimate theater company.

Deep Ellum Theatre Garage
501 2nd Ave., Bldg. A2
Dallas, TX 75226
(214) 826-3832
Alternative theater.

Fort Worth Theatre
3505 W. Lancaster Ave.
Fort Worth, TX 76107
(817) 738-1938
Community theater.

Garland Civic Theatre
1721 Reserve St.
Garland, TX 75042
(214) 349-1331
Community theater.

Hip Pocket Theatre
1627 Fairmount St.
Fort Worth, TX 76104
(817) 927-2833
Outdoor theater.

Richardson Theatre Center
2375 Promenade Center
Richardson, TX 75080
(214) 699-1130
Community theater.

Stage West
821 W. Vickery Blvd.
Fort Worth, TX 76104
(817) 332-6238
Legitimate theater.

Teatro Dallas
222 S. Montclair Ave.
Dallas, TX 75208
(214) 943-4429
Hispanic-American theater.

Theatre Arlington
1130 W. Division St.
Arlington, TX 76012
(817) 261-9628
Community theater.

Theatre Three
2800 Routh St., Suite 100
Dallas, TX 75201
(214) 871-3300
Legitimate theater.

BIOMEDICAL AND PHARMACEUTICALS

"If you want to be in biotechnology, you have to have the right academic training—chemistry or biochemistry—and three or four years' training time at a good research facility. Then you'll be in a good position for the future. As to the present, maybe in five years we'll have enough biotech companies to talk about. The science is here, but the industry is just developing."
Vin Protho, chairman, Dallas Biomedical Corp.

In large part because of the steady growth of the University of Texas Southwestern Medical Center in Dallas, biotechnology is one of the most promising new industries in the area—although it doesn't employ many workers yet.

166

Donations to Southwestern have boomed in recent years, thanks to the school's growing reputation as a research and teaching facility. Two researchers from the school won the Nobel Prize for medicine in 1985 and the Howard Hughes Medical Institute, the world's wealthiest medical philanthropic organization, is spending $20 million to develop a facility for molecular biology research at the center.

Add to that the creation of Dallas Biomedical, a unique venture that will match biomedical research with private investors to find marketable uses for existing research at Southwestern. The research may result in new drugs, therapeutic aids, processes, or instruments. If successful, the venture is expected to attract new biotech industries to Dallas and provide funds for continued research.

There are already several pharmaceutical laboratories in the area and more may follow if the biomedical industry continues to develop. Many of the nation's top pharmaceutical companies also have sales operations in the area.

Biomedical and pharmaceutical companies need biochemists, scientists, systems specialists, sales managers, and administrative and clerical workers. Biochemists and scientists will be in particularly heavy demand as the biotechnology industry develops.

Listed below are some of the area's largest biotechnology-related organizations, reflecting the variety of biomedical manufacturing and research. Information on other health care-related employers can be found in the "Health Care" section (page 180).

Abbott Laboratories
Diagnostic Division
1921 Hurd Dr.
Irving, TX 75038
(214) 518-6000
Designs, develops, and manufactures automated diagnostic instruments.

Alcon Laboratories Inc.
6201 S. Fwy.
Fort Worth, TX 76134
(817) 572-1361
Major manufacturer of ophthalmic products.

Carrington Laboratories Inc.
1300 E. Rochelle Blvd.
Irving, TX 75062
(214) 541-2278

Manufactures skin care products and conducts pharmaceutical research, including experimental AIDS drugs.

Dallas Biomedical Corp.
5420 LBJ Fwy., Suite 1265
Dallas, TX 75240
(214) 490-6711
Biotechnology venture capital group serving as matchmaker between researchers and investors to commercialize new biomedical techniques and processes.

Surgikos Inc.
2500 Arbrook Blvd.
Arlington, TX 76014
(817) 465-3141

Johnson & Johnson division that manufactures and markets specialty surgical products, including disposable packs and gowns, latex gloves, and antiseptics.

The University of Texas Southwestern Medical Center
5323 Harry Hines Blvd.
Dallas, TX 75235
(214) 688-3111
One of the nation's most prestigious medical research, patient care, and teaching schools.

BROADCASTING

Dallas is the center of the area's intensely competitive broadcasting industry. The major networks all have affiliates that maintain bureaus in both Dallas and Fort Worth and serve a wide area of north Texas. Dallas and Fort Worth also are served by two cable companies. More than forty radio stations provide a wide range of programming, including news and talk shows, sportscasts, easy listening, rock, country/western, classical, and jazz.

Because the area is one of the nation's top ten broadcasting markets, few people land jobs without experience. Working on a college radio or TV station helps, and some stations offer internships and part-time positions for people trying to get experience. But most broadcasting officials advise job hunters to go to a smaller market, work in as many areas as you can even if you have to volunteer, and learn how stations run. Area broadcasters routinely have openings for reporters, copywriters, advertising salespeople, and engineers with experience—but the competition is tough and you have to be aggressive and persistent.

Below is a sampling of the variety of radio and television companies, stations, and formats in the Dallas–Fort Worth area.

TELEVISION

Gaylord Broadcasting Co.
10111 N. Central Expwy.
Dallas, TX 75231
(214) 363-8722
Parent company of KTVT-TV Channel 11 in Fort Worth and other independent television stations.

KDAF-TV
8001 John Carpenter Fwy.
Dallas, TX 75247
Metro (214) 263-1140
Channel 33 independent television station.

KDFI-TV
433 Regal Row
Dallas, TX 75247
Metro (214) 263-8827
Channel 27 independent television station.

KDFW-TV
400 N. Griffin St.
Dallas, TX 75202
(214) 720-4444
Channel 4 CBS affiliate.

KDTN-TV
3000 Harry Hines Blvd.
Dallas, TX 75201
(214) 871-1390
Channel 2 educational.

KERA-TV
3000 Harry Hines Blvd.
Dallas, TX 75201
(214) 871-1390
Channel 13 public television for North Texas.

KTVT-TV
5233 Bridge St.
Fort Worth, TX 76103
Metro (817) 654-1100
Channel 11 independent television station.

KXAS-TV
3900 Barnett St.
Fort Worth, TX 76103
Metro (817) 429-1550
Channel 5 NBC affiliate.

WFAA-TV
Communications Center
606 Young St.
Dallas, TX 75202
(214) 748-9631
Channel 8 ABC affiliate.

CABLE

Cable News Network
1525 One Main Place
Dallas, TX 75202
(214) 747-1440
CNN news bureau.

Heritage Cablevision
6465 Jim Miller Rd.
Dallas, TX 75228
(214) 328-2882
Cable system serving Dallas, Farmers Branch, and Mesquite.

Sammons Communications
4528 W. Vickery Blvd.
Fort Worth, TX 76107
(817) 737-4731
Cable system serving Fort Worth.

RADIO

KERA-FM
3000 Harry Hines Blvd.
Dallas, TX 75201
(214) 871-1390
Public radio for North Texas.

KESS-FM
7700 John Carpenter Fwy.
Dallas, TX 75247
(214) 630-8531
Spanish-language radio.

KHYI-FM
545 E. John Carpenter Fwy.,
    Suite 1550
Irving, TX 75062
(214) 556-1195
Contemporary hits.

KKDA-FM
1230 River Bend, Suite 111
Dallas, TX 75247
(214) 634-7979
Urban contemporary.

KLIF-AM
3500 Maple Ave., Suite 1600
Dallas, TX 75219
(214) 526-2400
Talk radio.

KLTY-FM
7700 John Carpenter Fwy.
Dallas, TX 75247
(214) 263-0094
Adult Christian contemporary.

KOAI-FM
8235 Douglas Ave., Suite 300
Dallas, TX 75225
(214) 891-3400
Light jazz, light rock.

KPLX-FM
3500 Maple Ave., Suite 1600
Dallas, TX 75219
(214) 526-2400
Country.

KRLD-AM
1080 Metromedia Place
Dallas, TX 75247
(214) 634-1080
News and sports.

KVIL-FM
5307 E. Mockingbird La., Suite
  500
Dallas, TX 75206
(214) 826-7900
Adult contemporary.

KZEW-FM
3625 N. Hall St.
Dallas, TX 75219
(214) 748-9898
Album rock.

Texas State Network
7901 John Carpenter Fwy.
Dallas, TX 75247
(214) 688-1133
Statewide news network.

WBAP-AM
One Broadcast Hill
Fort Worth, TX 76103
Metro (817) 429-2330
Country.

WRR-FM
Fair Park Station
Dallas, TX 75226
(214) 670-8888
Classical.

EDUCATION

"There was a big buildup of Ph.D.s in the late 1950s because the Veterans Administration enabled people who had been in the military to get their educations paid for. Now the people who had been teaching thirty to thirty-five years are getting close to retirement. In the short term, the only place we can find American Ph.D.s is in companies."

> Bernie List, associate dean, Erik Jonsson School of Engineering and Computer Science, University of Texas at Dallas

Educational services, including all schools and colleges, public and private, will be one of the fastest growing sectors in the Dallas–Fort Worth job market in the 1990s.

The Texas Employment Commission projects the state will add about 180,000 new education jobs in the next fifteen years as a gradual shift toward higher-skilled professions will require more education and better language, math, and reasoning skills. Texas will also have a proportionally greater number of young people in school by the year 2000 than the United States as a whole, due mainly to the higher birth rates of the Hispanic population. Demand for bilingual teachers will be especially heavy.

Area elementary and secondary schools are already feeling the pinch. Many teachers have left the profession because of low pay. And the college and university professors hired during the post–World War II baby boom years when enrollment soared are now nearing retirement age. Engineering schools are already facing a shortage of Ph.D.s and are having to go to industry to find Ph.D.s to help teach graduate courses.

170

It all adds up to a seller's market for qualified people looking for jobs in education. Although teacher pay is still a big issue in the area—Texas ranks thirty-first in the country for average teacher salaries—there are moves under way to improve compensation.

Education also offers other types of jobs besides teaching. There are administrative, technical, and marketing positions as well.

The Dallas–Fort Worth area has an abundance of community colleges and private and public universities. The area also has several reputable trade schools that train workers for jobs in specific industries.

Several colleges and universities maintain hot lines with recorded listings of job openings. They include: Dallas County Community College District, (214) 746-2438; Southern Methodist University, (214) 692-2157; Tarrant County Junior College, (817) 877-9277; Texas Christian University, (817) 921-7791; the University of Texas at Arlington, metro (817) 273-3455; and the University of Texas at Dallas, (214) 690-2400.

Art Institute of Dallas
Two NorthPark East
8080 Park La.
Dallas, TX 75231
(214) 692-8080

Private two-year school offering associate degrees in commercial art, photography, interior design, fashion merchandising, music, and video.

Bauder Fashion College
508 S. Center St.
Arlington, TX 76010
(817) 277-6666

Private college offering two-year associate degrees in fashion merchandising, fashion design, and interior design.

Dallas Baptist University
7777 W. Kiest Blvd.
Dallas, TX 75211
Metro (214) 263-7595

Small private four-year liberal arts university with M.B.A. program and graduate programs in education and arts/biblical studies.

Dallas County Community College District
701 Elm St.
Dallas, TX 75202-3299
(214) 746-2149

Public two-year community college with seven campuses throughout the county and the Bill J. Priest Institute for Economic Development.

DeVry Institute of Technology
4250 N. Belt Line Rd.
Irving, TX 75038
(214) 258-6330

Private two-year college offering associate degrees in a variety of technical disciplines.

Southern Methodist University
Hillcrest and University
Dallas, TX 75275
(214) 692-2000

Large private four-year university with graduate programs, including an M.B.A. program and law school.

Tarrant County Junior College
District
1500 Houston St.
Fort Worth, TX 76102
(817) 336-7851
*Public two-year community col-
lege with three campuses.*

Texas Christian University
2800 S. University Dr.
Fort Worth, TX 76129
(817) 921-7000
*Large private four-year liberal
arts university with graduate
programs.*

Texas College of Osteopathic
Medicine
3500 Camp Bowie Blvd.
Fort Worth, TX 76107
(817) 735-2000
*Texas's only osteopathic medical
school.*

Texas Wesleyan College
1201 Wesleyan Dr.
Fort Worth, TX 76105
Metro (817) 429-8224
*Small private four-year liberal
arts university with graduate
programs in education and nursing anesthesiology.*

Texas Woman's University
P.O. Box 22939, TWU Station
Denton, TX 76204
(817) 898-2000
*Large private four-year coed uni-
versity with nursing school and
graduate programs.*

University of Dallas
1845 E. Northgate Dr.
Irving, TX 75062
(214) 721-5000

*Small private four-year liberal
arts university with graduate
programs in liberal arts and
management.*

University of North Texas
Ave. C. and Chestnut
Denton, TX 76203
Metro (817) 267-3731 or
(817) 565-2105
*Large public four-year university
with graduate programs.*

The University of Texas at
Arlington
800 S. Cooper St.
Arlington, TX 76019
(817) 273-2011
*Part of the University of Texas
system. Large public four-year
university with graduate programs and a robotics institute.*

The University of Texas at
Dallas
2601 N. Floyd Rd.
Richardson, TX 75080
(214) 690-2111
*Part of the University of Texas
system. Large public four-year
university with graduate
programs.*

The University of Texas Southwestern Medical Center
5323 Harry Hines Blvd.
Dallas, TX 75235
(214) 688-3111
*Part of the University of Texas
system. One of the most prestigious public medical schools in
the country for teaching, research, and patient care.*

ENGINEERING

Dallas–Fort Worth ranks as one of the top ten engineering
centers in the United States. The need for experienced engineers and engineering graduates is increasing, particularly
in the local high-technology industry.

Electrical engineers are among the most sought-after
professionals in the area. Most high-tech and telecommuni-

cations companies recruit heavily in colleges and look for experienced engineers for higher-level jobs. The University of Texas at Arlington, the University of Texas at Dallas, and Southern Methodist University have engineering schools that feed skilled workers to the local high-tech and engineering industries and offer graduate courses so engineers can continue and update their training.

The area's variety of industries has created a demand for engineers in a range of specialties: video, wastewater, quality assurance, mechanical, software support, design, systems, and new products. The area aerospace industry also has a strong need for manufacturing engineers who can design tooling and supervise the layout of increasingly automated plants.

Check the listings under "Aerospace and Defense," "High Technology," and "Telecommunications" for companies that employ large numbers of engineers in those fields. Some firms employ both architects and engineers, so also check the listing under "Architecture and Interior Design."

Below are some of Dallas–Fort Worth's engineering firms.

Albert H. Halff Associates Inc.
8616 Northwest Plaza Dr.
Dallas, TX 75225
(214) 739-0094

Black & Veatch
5728 LBJ Fwy., Suite 300
Dallas, TX 75240
(214) 770-1500

Bridgefarmer & Associates Inc.
1300 S. Sherman St., Suite 290
Richardson, TX 75081
(214) 231-8800

Carter & Burgess Inc.
  Engineers
1100 Macon St.
Fort Worth, TX 76102
(817) 335-2611

Cheatham & Associates
2011 E. Lamar Blvd., Suite 200
Arlington, TX 76006
(817) 460-2111

Freese & Nichols Inc.
811 Lamar St.
Fort Worth, TX 76102
(817) 336-7161

Greiner Engineering Inc.
909 E. Las Colinas Blvd.,
  Suite 1900
Irving, TX 75039
(214) 869-1001

Gruy Engineering Corp.
400 N. St Paul St., Suite 1300
Dallas, TX 75201
(214) 720-3800

Lockwood Greene Engineers
4201 Spring Valley Rd.,
  Suite 1500
Dallas, TX 75244
(214) 991-5505

Teague Nall and Perkins Inc.
915 Florence St.
Fort Worth, TX 76102
(817) 336-5773

Yandell & Hiller Inc.
301 Commerce St.
2100 City Center Tower II
Fort Worth, TX 76102
(317) 335-3000

ENTERTAINMENT/SPORTS

The Dallas–Fort Worth area offers a variety of entertainment and sports activities, from two-stepping in honky-tonks to cheering on the Dallas Cowboys. Organizations listed here aren't major employers, but they offer interesting jobs for the people who can get them.

Nightclubs primarily need wait-persons and bartenders, and they will sometimes hire extra people for big special events. Theme parks offer mainly seasonal employment and often hire students. Seasonal employment is also available at the annual State Fair of Texas in October, and Texas Stadium, the major stadium for the Dallas Cowboys and other events.

The professional sports teams don't need many more quarterbacks, goalies, pitchers, or guards, but they do look for clerical and administrative people.

Traditional networking probably won't pay off here, unless you, a friend, or a family member has a personal contact at one of the organizations. Just get your resume in and be persistent. And if you want a job at the Dallas Cowboys, it might help to know owner Jerry Jones!

NIGHTCLUBS

Billy Bob's Texas
2520 N. Commerce St.
Fort Worth, TX 76106
(817) 624-7117
World's largest honky-tonk.

Caravan of Dreams
312 Houston St.
Fort Worth, TX 76102
(817) 877-3000
Jazz/blues nightclub, theater, restaurant, bar.

Club Clearview
2806 Elm St.
Dallas, TX 75226
(214) 939-0006
Deep Ellum club featuring live music.

Dallas Alley
West End Marketplace
603 Munger Ave.
Dallas, TX 75202
(214) 954-4350
Collection of clubs featuring live bands.

The Venue
2727 Canton St.
Dallas, TX 75226
(214) 747-6336
Deep Ellum live music showcase club.

AMUSEMENTS/THEME PARKS

International Wildlife Park
601 Wildlife Pkwy.
Grand Prairie, TX 75050
Metro (214) 263-2203
Drive-through animal park.

Mesquite Arena
1818 Rodeo Dr.
Mesquite, TX 75149
(214) 285-8777
Weekly championship rodeo.

Palace of Wax and Ripley's
  Believe It or Not
601 E. Safari Pkwy.
Grand Prairie, TX 75050
Metro (214) 263-2391
Wax museum.

Six Flags Over Texas
2201 Road to Six Flags
Arlington, TX 76010
Metro (817) 640-8900
Family theme park.

Wet 'n Wild
Corporate Office
1901 N. Hwy. 360, Suite 111
Grand Prairie, TX 75050
(817) 640-8000
Family water park with locations in Arlington and Garland.

SPORTS

Dallas Cowboys
One Cowboys Pkwy.
Irving, TX 75063
(214) 556-9900
Professional football team.

Dallas Mavericks
777 Sports St.
Dallas, TX 75207
(214) 748-1808
Professional basketball team.

Dallas Sidekicks
6116 N. Central Expwy.,
   Suite 250
Dallas, TX 75206
(214) 361-5425
Professional soccer team.

Texas Rangers
1250 Copeland Rd., Suite 1100
Arlington, TX 76011
(817) 273-5222
Professional baseball team.

FOOD AND BEVERAGE

Manufacturing, selling, and distributing food and beverage products is a major industry in the Dallas–Fort Worth area. Snack food giant Frito-Lay has its national headquarters here, as do soft drink manufacturer Dr Pepper/Seven-Up and several national restaurant chains. Mexican food is an area manufacturing specialty, and several firms are in the beef-processing and meat-packing business.

For food and beverage distributors, the Dallas–Fort Worth area's central location provides easy access to huge markets in Texas and throughout the Southwest.

On the retail side, the area's food store chains have consolidated in recent years, and as a result, several large chains dominate the local market. Because the retailing side of the food and beverage industry is one of the first places to contract during depressed economic times as people cut back on expenses, some area food retailers and restaurants have suffered. But the Texas Employment Commission projects that eating and drinking places will add more than ninety thousand jobs by the year 2000 as the state's population grows, making food retailing one of the state's high-growth industries.

The food and beverage industry employs a variety of people. Distributors hire heavily in administrative and clerical areas. Retailers and manufacturers with national headquarters have jobs available in many different departments, including

175

finance, marketing, human resources, and public relations. Manufacturers also need production line workers, quality assurance specialists, and technicians to work in their plants.

Below is a sampling of the types of food and beverage companies operating in the area.

DISTRIBUTION

Affiliated Food Stores Inc.
100 Nat Gibbs Dr.
Keller, TX 76248
(817) 281-4417
Wholesale food distribution.

Ben E. Keith Co.
600 E. 9th St.
Fort Worth, TX 76102
(817) 654-3663
Food and beverage distribution.

White Swan Inc.
2700 Handley Ederville Rd
Fort Worth, TX 76118
(817) 284-4844
Food service distributor.

RETAILING

Chili's Inc.
6820 LBJ Fwy., Suite 200
Dallas, TX 75240
(214) 980-9917
Headquarters for national restaurant chain.

Cullum Cos.
14303 Inwood Rd.
Dallas, TX 75244
(214) 661-9700
Headquarters for operator of Tom Thumb/Page food and drug retail outlets.

El Chico Corp.
12200 Stemmons Fwy.,
    Suite 100
Dallas, TX 75234
(214) 241-5500
Headquarters for Mexican restaurant chain.

Kroger Co.
1901 Gateway Dr.
Dallas, TX 75038
(214) 580-3000

National retail food chain and food processor with locations throughout the area.

Minyard Food Stores Inc.
777 Freeport Pkwy.
Coppell, TX 75019
(214) 393-8700
Headquarters for retail and wholesale grocery chain.

Skaggs Alpha Beta
1100 Executive Dr., Suite 100
Richardson, TX 75081
(214) 238-7231
Major national retail food store chain with stores throughout the area.

The Southland Corp.
2828 N. Haskell Ave.
Dallas, TX 75204
(214) 828-7011
Corporate headquarters for 7-Eleven convenience stores and dairy products producer.

TGI Friday's Inc.
14665 Midway Rd.
Addison, TX 75244
(214) 450-5400
Headquarters for national restaurant chain.

Winn-Dixie Texas Inc.
5500 Hwy. 81 S.
Fort Worth, TX 76115
(817) 921-1100
Retail food store chain and dairy products producer with locations throughout Tarrant County.

MANUFACTURING

Design Foods
3709 E. 1st St.
Fort Worth, TX 76111
(817) 831-0981

Division of Sara Lee Corp. Manufactures and services food service industry.

Dr Pepper/Seven-Up Cos.
8144 Walnut Hill La.
Dallas, TX 75231-8144
(214) 360-7000

National headquarters for soft drink manufacturer and bottler.

Frito-Lay Inc.
7701 Legacy Dr.
Plano, TX 75024-4099
(214) 624-7000

National headquarters for snack food products manufacturer.

Miller Brewing Co.
7001 S. Fwy.
Fort Worth, TX 76134
(817) 551-3350

Texas's largest brewery.

MorningStar Foods Inc.
5956 Sherry La., Suite 1100
Dallas, TX 75225
(214) 360-4700

Dairy products manufacturer and distributor.

Mrs. Baird's Bakeries Inc.
5230 E. Mockingbird La.
Dallas, TX 75205
(214) 526-7201

Fort Worth plant:
7301 S. Fwy.
Fort Worth, TX 76134
(817) 293-5230

Bread and cake product manufacturer.

Rodriguez Festive Foods
913 N. Houston St.
Fort Worth, TX 76106
(817) 625-2831

Mexican foods manufacturer.

Supreme Beef Co.
5219 2nd Ave.
Dallas, TX 75210
(214) 428-1761

Beef processing plant.

GOVERNMENT

Government is one of the largest employers in the Dallas–Fort Worth area and it's growing even larger. The Texas Employment Commission estimates that about twenty-one thousand more people will be needed to work in government by 1995.

City and county governments are major employers in both Dallas and Fort Worth. Almost every federal agency has an office in one or both cities, many of them district or regional offices, and the federal government's presence continues to expand. Fort Worth, for example, beat out dozens of competitors to be chosen as the site for the Treasury Department's only U.S. currency plant outside Washington, D.C.

The Defense Department and the military services are especially large employers because of the area's concentration of defense contractors. The Defense Department has contract audit, investigative service, contract administration, quality assurance, and plant representative offices throughout the area.

Several military installations in the area employ both military and civilian workers. Carswell Air Force Base is the fourth largest employer in Fort Worth, with more than eight thousand workers, including about thirteen hundred civilians. Dallas is the world headquarters for the Army and Air Force Exchange Service, which directs domestic and overseas operations of the military services' retail and food service organization. AAFES employs thousands of civilians in a variety of jobs, including buyers, managerial, clerical, and warehouse positions.

Several government organizations provide recorded telephone job information lines. They include the City of Dallas, (214) 670-5908; the City of Fort Worth, (817) 870-7760; the Environmental Protection Agency, (214) 655-6538; the federal Office of Personnel Management, (214) 767-8035; and the U.S. Postal Service's main Dallas office, (214) 760-4531. A federal job opportunities list is also available at the Texas Employment Commission and is posted in federal courthouses. City job openings are often posted in public libraries.

If you're interested in working for the federal government, you also might want to check a bulletin of current federal job openings and federal job-related news published by Federal Job Information Services, a private Arlington company. For more information on the bulletin, see under "Libraries, Directories, and Publications."

Below are some of the types of government organizations in the area.

City Government

City governments need a variety of workers, including department administrators, financial analysts and planners, attorneys, librarians, real estate negotiators, public and community relations specialists, human services managers and counselors, police officers, firemen, data processing managers, and computer programmers—and, of course, city managers.

Although working for city government gives you visibility and lets you contribute directly to your community, keep in mind that city budgets are tight and salaries are usually lower than in private industry.

City of Arlington
101 W. Abram St.
Arlington, TX 76010
(817) 275-3271

City of Dallas
1500 Marilla St.
Dallas, TX 75201
(214) 670-3011

178

City of Fort Worth
1000 Throckmorton St.
Fort Worth, TX 76102
(817) 870-7750

City of Garland
200 N. 5th St.
Garland, TX 75040
(214) 205-2000

City of Irving
825 W. Irving Blvd.
Irving, TX 75060
(214) 721-2532

City of Plano
1612 Ave. K
Plano, TX 75074
(214) 424-6531

City of Richardson
411 W. Arapaho Rd.
Richardson, TX 75080
(214) 238-4100

County Government

County governments offer jobs in law, human services, public health, and tax accounting. County governments have an extensive court system, so many jobs are law-oriented—attorneys, clerks, and secretaries. County human services departments also employ social workers, counselors, and administrators. And counties are the government entities that appraise property and assess and collect taxes, so they need appraisers and accountants.

Dallas County
600 Commerce St.
Dallas, TX 75202
(214) 653-7011

Tarrant County
100 E. Weatherford St.
Fort Worth, TX 76196
(317) 334-1111

Federal Government

Federal government agencies have a wide range of job opportunities, including contract specialists, engineers, technicians, coordinators, nurses, police officers, inspectors, and auditors.

Army and Air Force Exchange
  Service
3911 S. Walton Walker Blvd.
Dallas, TX 75236
(214) 780-2011

Army Corps of Engineers
District Office
819 Taylor St.
Fort Worth, TX 76102
(817) 334-2300

Carswell Air Force Base
Fort Worth, TX 76127
(817) 782-5000

Defense Contract Audit Agency
1100 Commerce St., Room
  3B17
Dallas, TX 75242-0397
(214) 767-0458

Environmental Protection
  Agency
Regional Headquarters
1445 Ross Ave.
Dallas, TX 75202
(214) 655-6560

Federal Aviation
   Administration
Southwest Regional
   Headquarters
4400 Blue Mound Rd.
Fort Worth, TX 76106
(817) 624-5000

Naval Air Station–Dallas
Dallas, TX 75211
(214) 266-6111

U.S. Postal Service
Main Office–Dallas
401 Interstate 30
Dallas, TX 75260
(214) 760-4531

U.S. Postal Service
Main Post Office–Fort Worth
4600 Mark IV Pkwy.
Fort Worth, TX 76161
(817) 625-3366

State Government

The State of Texas hires many types of workers for state commissions and agencies, including administrators, investigators, auditors, social workers, nurses, rehabilitation specialists, and clerks.

Fort Worth State School
5000 Campus Dr.
Fort Worth, TX 76119
(817) 534-4831

Texas Dept. of Human Services
Administrative Office
631 106th St.
Arlington, TX 76011
Metro (817) 640-5090

Texas Employment
   Commission
8300 John Carpenter Fwy.
Dallas, TX 75356-9460
(214) 631-6050

Texas Rehabilitation
   Commission
Dallas Regional Office
10935 Estate La. Suite 370
Dallas, TX 75238
(214) 343-0991

HEALTH CARE

"There will be more demand for patient services by virtue of the growth of the community and changing demographics. If we are successful in positioning this area as a referral center and encourage the development of new techniques and technologies, that in turn will generate a whole host of job opportunities. Our goal is to establish Dallas as a medical mecca by the twenty-first century."
                    Frank J. Weaver, executive director and chief
                    executive officer, Dallas Medical Action Group

Health care services is expected to show the strongest employment growth of any area industry during the next fifteen years. The Texas Employment Commission predicts health services will add two hundred thousand jobs—a whopping 48 percent increase—throughout the state by the year 2000.

Dallas–Fort Worth, one of the state's major health care and teaching centers, will gobble up a significant portion of those new jobs. The University of Texas Southwestern Medical

School in Dallas is growing in prestige, several hospitals are expanding, and the area is gaining a reputation in specializations such as organ transplants. In addition, the medical school and eight major medical facilities in Dallas have joined forces in the Dallas Medical Action Group, a nonprofit organization that aims to position the area as a major medical referral center.

As baby boomers age, the increasingly older population in Dallas–Fort Worth will require more health care services, particularly nursing homes and home care workers. The TEC predicts jobs in the most demand in the next fifteen years will be for registered nurses, nursing aides, orderlies, and home health aides.

Health care is also employing an increasing number of managers in the Dallas–Fort Worth area. Many local hospitals own and operate several different hospitals, each requiring an administrative staff. The largest hospital in Dallas, Baylor University Medical Center, employs more than six thousand people and has five affiliate hospitals. The largest hospital in Forth Worth, Harris Hospital–Methodist. employs almost five thousand people and has ten hospitals in its health system.

Dallas–Fort Worth also has many health care companies that own and manage a variety of hospitals, clinics, and nursing homes. They require managerial staffs, as do health maintenance organizations and preferred provider organizations.

The Dallas–Fort Worth area, like other parts of the country, is facing a critical shortage of nurses. Most advertised positions are for nurses, but health care organizations are also hiring compensation analysts, community professional liaisons, medical technicians, pharmacists, therapists, social workers, and clerical workers. In addition to hospitals and clinics, private companies also hire occupational nurses.

The following is a selective listing of the area's health care organizations.

Hospitals

All Saints Episcopal Hospital
1400 8th Ave.
Fort Worth, TX 76104
(817) 926-2544

Arlington Memorial Hospital
800 W. Randol Mill Rd.
Arlington, TX 76012
Metro (817) 265-5581

Baylor University Medical
 Center
3500 Gaston Ave.
Dallas, TX 75246
(214) 820-0111

Children's Medical Center
 Dallas
1935 Motor St.
Dallas, TX 75235
(214) 920-2000

HCA Medical Center of Plano
3901 W. 15th St.
Plano, TX 75075
(214) 596-6800

John Peter Smith Hospital
1500 S. Main St.
Fort Worth, TX 76104
(817) 921-3431

Harris Hospital–H.E.B.
1600 Hospital Pkwy.
Bedford, TX 76022
Metro (817) 267-3956

Memorial Hospital of Garland
2300 Marie Curie Dr.
Garland, TX 75042
(214) 487-5000

Harris Hospital–Methodist
1325 Pennsylvania Ave.
Fort Worth, TX 76104
(817) 882-2000

Parkland Memorial Hospital
5201 Harry Hines Blvd.
Dallas, TX 75235
(214) 590-8000

Irving Healthcare System
1901 N. MacArthur Blvd.
Irving, TX 75061
(214) 579-8100

Richardson Medical Center
401 W. Campbell Rd.
Richardson, TX 75080
(214) 231-1441

Health Care Companies

Health care companies own and manage groups of hospitals. Some also have clinics, nursing homes, and other health care providers under their corporate umbrella. They employ mainly administrative workers who oversee central functions such as finance and marketing. The area's largest health care organizations follow.

Epic Health Care Group
433 E. Las Colinas Blvd.,
   Suite 500
Irving, TX 75039
(214) 869-0707

Volunteer Hospitals of
   America Inc.
5215 N. O'Connor Rd.
Irving, TX 75039
(214) 830-0000

Republic Health Corp.
15303 Dallas Pkwy., Suite 1400
Dallas, TX 75248
(214) 851-3100

Cooperative owned by not-for-profit hospitals.

Health Maintenance Organizations

Health maintenance organizations control where their clients are going to receive health care services. In return, the health care providers participating in the plan offer their services at discount rates, thus controlling costs.

Area HMOs are growing rapidly. Most have multiple locations throughout the area, each employing physicians, nurses, technicians, and other medical personnel. HMO administrative offices also hire a variety of clerical, data entry, financial, and marketing employees to administer the plans.

The following are some of the area's fastest growing HMOs.

Cigna Healthplan of Texas Inc.
600 Las Colinas Blvd.
Irving, TX 75039
(214) 869-8700

Kaiser Permanente
12720 Hillcrest Rd., Suite 600
Dallas, TX 75230
(214) 458-5000

Harris Methodist Health Plan
    Inc.
1325 Pennsylvania Ave.
Fort Worth, TX 76104
(817) 878-5800

Sanus Texas Health Plan Inc.
3600 Freeport Pkwy.,
    Suite 3040
Irving, TX 75063
Metro (214) 621-8143

Preferred Provider Organizations

Preferred provider organizations, or PPOs, offer a select network of hospitals and health care providers to control health care costs. Some are cosponsored by hospitals and insurance companies.

In addition to administrators who oversee the program, PPOs employ a professional staff including nurses and nursing educators. More and more corporations are beginning to form their own PPOs to control their medical insurance costs.

The following are some of the area's largest PPOs.

North Texas Healthcare
    Network
5605 N. MacArthur Blvd.,
    Suite 520
Irving, TX 75038
Metro (214) 751-0047

Trinity Health Network
1307 8th Ave.
Fort Worth, TX 76104
(817) 921-1629

Partners National Health Plans
5215 N. O'Connor Rd.
Irving, TX 75039
(214) 869-2500

HIGH TECHNOLOGY

"Texas Instruments hires eight hundred to a thousand college graduates every year, principally engineering personnel. Ninety percent are in electrical engineering, computer science, industrial engineering, and mechanical engineering though we also hire in control and finance. We mainly hire at the entry level and promote from within. We don't have a formal training program. People get on-the-job training. We also hire a lot of people on the basis of resumes. Don't be afraid to write in. We do work the paper very hard. A good resume means a lot."

George Berryman, manager of college recruiting,
Texas Instruments Inc.

Dallas–Fort Worth is home to almost a thousand high-tech companies, from one- and two-person research labs to giants like Texas Instruments Inc., which employs about thirty-five thousand area workers. The area is known locally as the "Silicon Prairie" because of its conglomeration of computer, software, electronics, and telecommunications companies. Only California's famed Silicon Valley and Boston's Route 128 are said to have larger high-tech industries.

The heaviest concentration of high-tech companies lies along the so-called "Richardson corridor," stretching from LBJ Freeway through Richardson and north to Plano. Another cluster of high-tech companies lies in Las Colinas, a planned business and residential development near Dallas/Fort Worth International Airport. Still others are scattered throughout the suburbs and west to Arlington and Fort Worth, headquarters of Tandy.

The Dallas–Fort Worth high-tech industry is nationally known for its work in artificial intelligence, voice-activated systems, electro-optics, and specialized silicon chips. The variety of high-tech jobs available ranges from researchers experimenting with new technologies to production workers fabricating silicon wafers in sterile environments. Electrical engineers are in highest demand, along with computer scientists.

Many companies hire most of their engineers right out of college for entry-level positions, then give them on-the-job training and promote from within. There also is strong demand for technicians, many of whom are hired from local junior colleges and trade schools that have electronics programs.

Area corporations in a variety of fields also need in-house systems analysts, programmers, and data processing managers.

The high-tech industry is closely allied with area colleges and universities. It depends on these institutions for new talent and continuing education for its engineers, whose training rapidly becomes obsolete. Engineering schools at the University of Texas at Arlington, the University of Texas at Dallas, and Southern Methodist University work closely with high-tech companies to develop programs and place students. Many companies hire college students part-time or for internship programs.

The Texas chapter of the American Electronics Association is very active locally and offers good networking opportunities for electronics professionals and managers. The AEA holds monthly programs that are open to any interested person for a fee, and publishes a national directory of high-tech companies with geographic cross-references. For more information about the AEA's services, see the section "Business Networks and Professional Organizations."

Texas Instruments also has its own recorded job bank of openings. The hot line number is (214) 995-6666.

The following is a sampling of the area's high-tech companies, including large firms as well as some up-and-coming start-ups. In addition to the firms listed below, many major computer and electronics companies maintain division administrative or regional sales offices in the area. IBM has an important sales and service presence locally and also develops software.

Telecommunications companies are listed separately on page 206 and defense electronics companies can be found in the "Aerospace and Defense" list on page 158.

COMPUTERS—
DATA PROCESSING

Affiliated Computer Systems Inc.
2828 N. Haskell
Dallas, TX 75204
(214) 733-6185
On-line transaction processing services.

Computer Language Research Inc.
2395 Midway Rd.
Carrollton, TX 75006
(214) 250-7000
Computerized tax processing services.

Cronus Industries Inc.
1111 W. Mockingbird La.,
    Suite 1400
Dallas, TX 75247
(214) 905-2590
Information processing services.

Electronic Data Systems Corp.
Staffing Office
12200 Park Central Dr.,
    Suite 200
Dallas, TX 75251
(214) 661-6000
Wholly owned subsidiary of General Motors. Computer design, programming, consulting, and

operation for corporate and government customers.

Policy Management Systems
12377 Merit Dr.
Dallas, TX 75251-0785
(214) 233-9309
Software and data processing services to the insurance industry.

COMPUTERS—
MANUFACTURING

Convex Computer Corp.
300 Waterview Pkwy.
Richardson, TX 75080
(214) 497-4000
Headquarters for designer of supercomputer systems.

Tandy Corp.
100 Throckmorton St.
Fort Worth, TX 76102
(817) 390-3700
Headquarters for computer and consumer electronics manufacturer and retailer.

VITec Inc.
3460 Lotus Dr.
Plano, TX 75075
(214) 596-5600
Designs and develops graphics image-processing computer and display systems.

185

ELECTRONIC COMPONENT DESIGNERS AND MANUFACTURERS

American Medical Electronics Inc.
4125 Keller Springs Rd., Suite 144
Dallas, TX 75244
(214) 248-6000
Medical equipment, bone growth stimulators.

BancTec Inc.
4435 Spring Valley Rd.
Dallas, TX 75244
(214) 450-7700
Image recognition systems for processing financial transaction documents.

Clini-Therm Corp.
12046 Forestgate Dr.
Dallas, TX 75243
(214) 669-2707
Computer-controlled hyperthermia systems for cancer treatment.

Collmer Semiconductor Inc.
14368 Proton Rd.
Dallas, TX 75244
(214) 233-1589
Electronic components, semiconductor devices, high-voltage power assemblies.

Dallas Semiconductor Corp.
4350 Beltwood Pkwy. S.
Dallas, TX 75244-3219
(214) 450-0400
Specialized computer chips.

ElectroCom Automation Inc.
2910 Ave. F
Arlington, TX 76011-5276
(817) 640-5690
Document processing equipment, mobile radios, voice and data transmission systems.

Environmental Processing Inc.
1331 N. Plano Rd.
Richardson, TX 75081
(214) 669-0830
Semiconductor condition and test.

Fared Robot Systems Inc.
7410 Pebble Dr.
Fort Worth, TX 76118
(817) 284-3401
Factory automation equipment.

General Instrument Corp.
Tocom Division
3301 Royalty Row
Irving, TX 75062
(214) 438-7691
Converters and descramblers, interactive cable television systems and equipment, cable security systems.

Honeywell Inc.
Optoelectronics Division
830 E. Arapaho Rd.
Richardson, TX 75081
(214) 234-4271
Optoelectronic components and assemblies.

Interphase Corp.
2925 Merrell Rd.
Dallas, TX 75229
(214) 350-9000
Computer disc, tape, and communications controllers.

Multimil Inc.
670 International Pkwy., Suite 190
Richardson, TX 75081
(214) 644-7724
Smart cards.

National Semiconductor Corp.
1111 W. Bardin Rd.
Arlington, TX 76017
(817) 468-6300
Integrated circuits.

Recognition Equipment Inc.
2701 E. Grauwyler Rd.
Irving, TX 75061
(214) 579-6000
Optical character recognition systems for document handling and computer data entry.

Rockwell International Corp.
Electronics Operations
1200 N. Alma Rd.
Richardson, TX 75081
(214) 996-5000
Commercial electronics.

Scientific Communications Inc.
2908 National Dr.
Garland, TX 75041
(214) 840-4900

Receivers, amplifiers, voltage control oscillators, components.

SGS Thomson Microelectronics Inc.
1310 Electronics Dr.
Carrollton, TX 75006
(214) 466-6000

Integrated circuits.

Spectradyne Inc.
1501 N. Plano Rd.
Richardson, TX 75081
(214) 234-2721

Pay-per-view movie and video systems for hotels.

STB Systems, Inc.
1651 N. Glenville, Suite 210
Richardson, TX 75081
(214) 234-8750

Memory expansion boards for IBM computers.

Teledyne Geotech
3401 Shiloh Rd.
Garland, TX 75041
(214) 271-2561

Earth sciences data gathering, detection, and measurement equipment.

Texas Instruments Inc.
13500 N. Central Expwy.
Dallas, TX 75243
(214) 995-2011

Worldwide headquarters for designer and manufacturer of integrated circuits, microelectronic components, computer systems, consumer electronics.

Varian Continental Electronics
4212 S. Buckner Blvd.
Dallas, TX 75227
(214) 381-7161

Broadcast and special purpose transmitters.

Voice Control Systems
14140 Midway Rd., Suite 100
Dallas, TX 75244
(214) 386-0300

Voice recognition products.

SOFTWARE DEVELOPERS

Computer Associates International Inc.
909 E. Las Colinas Blvd.
Irving, TX 75039
(214) 556-7100

Mainframe systems and banking applications software. Formerly Uccel Corp.

Computrac Inc.
222 Municipal Dr.
Richardson, TX 75080
(214) 234-4241

Turnkey computer systems and software for the legal market.

DAC Software
17950 Preston Rd.
Dallas, TX 75252
(214) 248-0205

Accounting software, personal computer equipment.

Hogan Systems Inc.
5080 Spectrum Dr.
Dallas, TX 75248
(214) 386-0020

Applications systems for the financial industry.

International Business Machines Corp.
Central Employment Office
P.O. Box 819042
Dallas, TX 75381-9042
(214) 620-6683

Software development, marketing, and service area offices.

Shared Financial Systems Inc.
15301 Dallas Pkwy., Suite 600
Dallas, TX 75248
(214) 233-8356

Computer banking software.

Sterling Software Inc.
8080 N. Central Expwy.,
  Suite 1100
Dallas, TX 75206
(214) 891-8600

Software products and services for financial industry and government.

HOTELS/MOTELS

Dallas is the nation's third leading destination for conventions behind New York City and Chicago, hosting more than 2 million convention guests annually. The area also ranks as one of the state's top tourist destinations, and Dallas/Fort Worth International Airport draws business travelers from around the world.

The combination translates into big business for area hotels. More than two hundred hotels serve Dallas–Fort Worth, and more are under construction. Major hotel and motel chains, including Doubletree, Harvey, Hilton, Holiday Inn, Hyatt Regency, Marriott, and Sheraton, have multiple locations throughout the area. The larger hotels employ anywhere from one hundred to two thousand workers at one location.

The area also is headquarters for several major hotel and motel companies: Integra, a hotel and restaurant company; Pratt Hotel Corp., a casino and hotel management company; and Motel 6 L.P., operator of the Motel 6 motel chain.

Hotels and motels need a variety of part-time and full-time service workers, from housekeepers, food servers, and bellpersons to more skilled positions such as auditors, banquet managers, engineers, accounting clerks, concierges, and restaurant managers. Most hotels want job seekers to apply in person and require at least two years of experience for any kind of managerial position. Because the area is host to so many conventions, catering sales is a major part of many hotels' operations and offers high visibility and particularly good opportunities for advancement.

The following is a sampling of the area's hotels, including new ones in the suburbs as well as the grand old hotels in the downtown areas. Hotel companies are also listed.

HOTELS

The Adolphus
1321 Commerce St.
Dallas, TX 75202
(214) 742-8200

Crescent Court Hotel
400 Crescent Ct.
Dallas, TX 75201
(214) 871-3200

DFW Hilton Executive Conference Center
1800 E. Hwy. 26
Grapevine, TX 76051
(817) 481-8444

Doubletree Hotel–Park West
1590 LBJ Fwy.
Dallas, TX 75234
(214) 869-4300

Fairmont Hotel
1717 N. Akard St.
Dallas, TX 75201
(214) 720-2020

Four Seasons Resort & Club
4150 N. MacArthur Blvd.
Irving, TX 75062
(214) 717-0700

Harvey Hotel–Addison
14315 Midway Rd.
Addison, TX 75244
(214) 980-8877

Hyatt Regency Dallas
300 Reunion Blvd.
Dallas, TX 75240
(214) 651-1234

Hyatt Regency Fort Worth
815 Main St.
Fort Worth, TX 76102
(817) 870-1234

Loews Anatole Hotel
2201 Stemmons Fwy.
Dallas, TX 75207
(214) 748-1200

The Mansion on Turtle Creek
2821 Turtle Creek Blvd.
Dallas, TX 75219
(214) 559-2100

Marriott Mandalay at Las
  Colinas
221 E. Las Colinas Blvd.
Irving, TX 75039
(214) 556-0800

Park Inn Plaza
1914 Commerce St.
Dallas, TX 75201
(214) 747-7000

Sheraton Centrepark Hotel
1500 Convention Center Dr.
Arlington, TX 76011
(817) 261-8200

Westin Hotel Galleria
13340 Dallas Pkwy.
Dallas, TX 75240
(214) 934-9494

Worthington Hotel
200 Main St.
Fort Worth, TX 76102
(817) 870-1000

HOTEL COMPANIES

Integra—A Hotel and Restaurant Co.
4441 W. Airport Fwy.
Irving, TX 75015
(214) 258-8500
*Hotels and food service. For-
merly Brock Hotel Corp.*

Motel 6 L.P.
14651 Dallas Pkwy.
Dallas, TX 75240
(214) 386-6161
National motel chain.

Pratt Hotel Corp.
Two Galleria Tower, Suite 2200
13455 Noel Rd.
Dallas, TX 75240
(214) 386-9777
Casino and hotel management.

HUMAN SERVICES

Human services is a field where you can be challenged profes-
sionally and at the same time feel that you are contributing
to the well-being of others. It's also an area that is expanding
beyond social service agencies into corporations and government.

Dallas and Fort Worth are sites of several national, regional,
or district offices for many human services organizations that
hire counselors, social workers, volunteer coordinators, psychologists, nurses, rehabilitation specialists, and others.
Headquarters operations also employ administrators and
lobbyists.

Volunteers are almost always welcome in such organiza-

189

tions. Many groups train volunteers, a good way to get started in a human services career. See under "Career Exploration and Training Opportunities" for information about volunteer organizations and training.

Most large hospitals have social services departments that provide services such as community education, substance abuse units, hospice programs, bereavement support groups, and rehabilitation programs. City, county, and federal governments have human services departments that provide financial assistance, counseling, housing, and other services for needy residents.

Keep in mind that corporate human resources departments are increasingly providing or coordinating referral programs for their employees. These employee assistance programs can include marriage and family counseling and substance abuse counseling.

The list that follows includes some of the human services employers in the Dallas–Fort Worth area. Two good sources for comprehensive lists of organizations are the United Way of Metropolitan Tarrant County's "blue book" of human services agencies and the Community Council of Greater Dallas's directory of social service organizations. See under "Libraries, Directories, and Publicatons" for more information about these directories.

American Cancer Society
2222 Montgomery St.
Fort Worth, TX 76107
(214) 737-3185
Texas division office of national association that provides equipment, transportation to treatment centers, information, referral and guidance, and support groups.

American Diabetes Association
  Texas Affiliate Inc.
8440 Walnut Hill La., Suite 260
Dallas, TX 75231
(214) 692-6434
North Texas regional office of national association that seeks to control diabetes, provide education, and support research.

Association for Retarded
  Citizens
2501 Ave. J
Arlington, TX 76005
Metro (817) 640-0204

National headquarters for organization providing socialization programming, parental counseling, aid to families in finding services, day care, and lobbying for legislation.

Edna Gladney Center
2300 Hemphill St.
Fort Worth, TX 76110
(817) 926-3304
Adoption and social services.

Expanco Inc.
3005 Wichita Ct.
Fort Worth, TX 76140
(817) 293-9486
Provides controlled working environments for those not employable in normal industry.

Family Service Inc.
1424 Hemphill St.
Fort Worth, TX 76104
(817) 927-8884
Counseling services.

190

Goodwill Industries of Dallas
2800 N. Hampton Rd.
Dallas, TX 75212
(214) 638-2800

Goodwill Industries of Fort
  Worth Inc.
1701 E. Lancaster Ave.
Fort Worth, TX 76102
(817) 332-7866
*Provides vocational rehabilita-
tion for physically and mentally
disabled and economically
disadvantaged.*

Lighthouse for the Blind
4245 Office Pkwy.
Dallas, TX 75204
(214) 821-2375
*Provides training, vocational
evaluation, and sheltered employment for the visually impaired.*

Mothers Against Drunk Driving
  (MADD)
669 Airport Fwy., Suite 310
Hurst, TX 76053
(817) 268-6233
*National headquarters for associ-
ation that lobbies for tougher legislation against drinking and
driving and seeks to educate the
public on the issue.*

Senior Citizens of Greater Dallas Inc.
2905 Swiss Ave.
Dallas, TX 75204
(214) 823-5700

Senior Citizens of Greater Tarrant County
1000 Macon St.
Fort Worth, TX 76102
(817) 338-4433
*Provides recreational and educa-
tion activities for people fifty-five
years of age and over, volunteer
activities, referrals to other agencies, health screenings, and legal
information.*

Texas Dept. of Human Services
Regional Administrative Office
631 106th St.
Arlington, TX 76011
(817) 540-5090
*State agency that oversees Aid to
Families with Dependent Children program, food stamp program, child protective services,
day care licensing service, aged
and disabled services, and food
services for children.*

United Way of Metropolitan
  Dallas
901 Ross Ave.
Dallas, TX 75202
(214) 720-1801

United Way of Metropolitan
  Tarrant County
210 E. 9th St.
Fort Worth, TX 76102
(817) 878-0000
*Provides support for health, fam-
ily, child care and personal development agencies and services
that have been approved and ac-
cepted for affiliation by a board
of directors.*

INSURANCE

The Dallas–Fort Worth area is one of the nation's insurance
centers. In fact, locals used to boast that Dallas had more
insurance company home offices than any other city except
Hartford, Connecticut. Headquarters operations include Employers Insurance of Texas, United Group Association, and
National Foundation Life Insurance.

A variety of insurance companies operate in the area: life,
medical and health, fire, marine and casualty, surety, title,

pension, health and welfare funds. Almost every major national insurer has several local offices. Blue Cross and Blue Shield and State Farm Mutual Insurance are among the area's top hundred employers.

The insurance industry employs agents as well as brokers, business analysts, claims examiners, legal assistants, underwriters, customer service representatives, sales personnel, commercial raters, adjusters, and clerical workers. In addition, headquarters operations offer job opportunities in finance and administration. Financial institutions also hire collateral and insurance clerks to monitor credit life files on consumer loans.

The listing below provides a sampling of the area's insurance companies.

Alexander & Alexander of Texas Inc.
717 N. Harwood St.
Dallas, TX 75201
(214) 880-0321

Blue Cross and Blue Shield of Texas Inc.
901 S. Central Expwy.
Richardson, TX 75080
(214) 669-6900

Crum & Forster
4040 N. Central Expwy.
Dallas, TX 75204
(214) 827-6110

Employers Insurance of Texas
1301 Young St.
Dallas, TX 75202
(214) 760-6100

Fidelity Union Life Insurance Co.
2323 Bryan St.
Dallas, TX 75201
(214) 978-7000

Houston General Insurance Group
4055 International Plaza
Fort Worth, TX 76109
(817) 731-7313

Marsh & McLennan Cos. Inc.
2121 San Jacinto St.,
  Suite 1300
Dallas, TX 75201
(214) 979-9900

Millers Insurance Group
300 Burnett St.
Fort Worth, TX 76102
(817) 332-7761

National Farm Life Insurance Co.
6001 Bridge St.
Fort Worth, TX 76102
(817) 451-9550

National Foundation Life Insurance Co.
777 Main St.
Fort Worth, TX 76102
(817) 877-3717

Southwestern Life Insurance Co.
500 N. Akard St.
Dallas, TX 75201
(214) 954-7111

Transport Life Insurance Co.
714 Main St.
Fort Worth, TX 76102
(817) 390-8000

United Group Association
5215 N. O'Connor Rd.,
  Suite 1800
Irving, TX 75039
(214) 869-4800

INVESTMENT BANKERS AND BROKERS

The investment business in Dallas–Fort Worth has been more cautious and conservative in its hiring in recent years as bull markets turned into bears. But there are still opportunities for job hunters in the investment business, and technology is creating many of them.

Because computer networks are so important in communicating between offices and receiving market data, investment companies are hiring heavily in the systems area—analysts, programmers, and designers, for example. Investment companies also still need sales and service people, communications managers, and data entry and clerical personnel.

Many large investment firms recruit at area colleges and universities and put entry-level employees through extensive training programs. Most other jobs require several years' experience. Some investment firms are beginning to offer internships more frequently for very specific jobs tailored to the individual.

Listed below are some local investment bankers and brokers. Most well-known Wall Street firms maintain offices in both Dallas and Fort Worth as well as in the suburbs. In addition, several regional firms service the area. Because so many large firms have multiple locations, only their main downtown Dallas and Fort Worth offices are listed. Those offices can refer you to the localities.

A. G. Edwards & Sons Inc.
100 One Main Place
Dallas, TX 75201
(214) 741-7911

Fort Worth office:
1701 River Run
Fort Worth, TX 76107
(817) 338-1401

Dean Witter Reynolds Inc.
2300 Lincoln Plaza
500 N. Akard St.
Dallas, TX 75201
(214) 740-2000

Fort Worth office:
201 Main St., Suite 1500
Fort Worth, TX 76102
(817) 332-6700

Donaldson Lufkin Jenrette
2200 Ross Ave.
2900 Texas Commerce Tower
Dallas, TX 75201
Metro (214) 263-3646

Drexel Burnham Lambert Inc.
300 Crescent Ct., Suite 1600
Dallas, TX 75201
(214) 969-4030

Eppler Guerin & Turner Inc.
1445 Ross Ave., Suite 2300
Dallas, TX 75202
(214) 380-9000

Fort Worth office:
306 W. 7th St., Suite 600
Fort Worth, TX 76102
(817) 335-2571

Fidelity Investments Southwest
400 E. Las Colinas Blvd.
Irving, TX 75039
(214) 830-7000

Kidder Peabody & Co. Inc.
1201 Elm St., Suite 3939
Dallas, TX 75270
(214) 761-7000

Merrill Lynch Pierce Fenner &
Smith Inc.
2121 San Jacinto St.,
Suite 1200
Dallas, TX 75201
(214) 969-0008

Fort Worth office:
201 Main St., Suite 850
Fort Worth, TX 76102
(817) 335-3751

PaineWebber
1601 Elm St.
Dallas, TX 75201
(214) 978-6000

Fort Worth office:
301 Commerce St., Suite 2800
Fort Worth, TX 76102
Metro (817) 429-0248

Prudential-Bache Securities
10440 N. Central Expwy.,
Suite 1600
Dallas, TX 75231
(214) 373-2700

Fort Worth office:
777 Taylor St.
Fort Worth, TX 76102
(817) 336-8701

Rausher Pierce Refsnes Inc.
700 N. Pearl St.
2500 RPR Tower
Dallas, TX 75201
(214) 978-0111

Fort Worth office:
6300 Ridglea Place, Suite 100
Fort Worth, TX 76116
(817) 737-7242

Rotan Mosle Inc.
1201 Elm St.
2600 Renaissance Tower
Dallas, TX 75270
(214) 651-6000

Shearson Lehman Hutton Inc.
1999 Bryan St.
Dallas, TX 75201
(214) 979-7000

Fort Worth office:
1320 S. University Dr.,
Suite 1000
Fort Worth, TX 76107
(817) 336-7891

Smith Barney Harris Upham &
Co. Inc.
200 Crescent Ct., Suite 1200
Dallas, TX 75201
(214) 855-7900

Weber Hall Sale & Associates
Inc.
1525 Elm St., Suite 1800
Dallas, TX 75201
(214) 954-9472

LAW

While some law firms have been hurt by the economy and
their clients' financial prob ems, others are still improving
their profits by serving the area's changing legal needs.

Many firms are doing more bankruptcy and litigation work
as a result of the tough economic times. Firms that once
helped put together deals in the real estate business are now
getting involved in workouts of problem loans. For example,
while only a handful of local lawyers practiced bankruptcy
law full-time in the 1960s, about five hundred attorneys now
practice in the Dallas Bar Association's bankruptcy section.

Large firms with more than a hundred local lawyers recruit heavily from law schools, particularly for graduates at the top of their class. Many firms also are making more lateral hires. Mobility has hit the legal profession; the days are gone when an attorney joined a firm and stayed there for the rest of his or her career. Area firms also are making a much stronger push to hire minorities.

Law firms hire people other than lawyers. They need clerical workers, paralegals, proofreaders, and secretaries. They also employ certified public accountants, business managers, and marketing specialists.

The list below includes some of the area's largest firms, as well as some smaller firms that have the potential to grow.

Cantey & Hanger
801 Cherry St.
Fort Worth, TX 76102
(817) 877-2800

Gandy Michener Swindle
  Whitaker & Pratt
2501 Parkview Dr., Suite 600
Fort Worth, TX 76102
Metro (817) 429-6268 or
  (817) 335-4417

Gardere & Wynne
717 N. Harwood St.
Dallas, TX 75201
(214) 979-4500

Hughes & Luce
1717 Main St.
Dallas, TX 75201
(214) 939-5500

Jenkins & Gilchrist
1445 Ross Ave., Suite 3200
Dallas, TX 75202
(214) 855-4500

Johnson & Gibbs
900 Jackson St.
Dallas, TX 75202
(214) 977-9000

Kelly, Hart & Hallman
201 Main St., Suite 2500
Fort Worth, TX 76102
(817) 332-2500

Law, Snakard & Gambill
3200 Texas American Bank
  Bldg.
Fort Worth, TX 76102
Metro (817) 429-2991 or
  (817) 335-7373

Locke Purnell Rain Harrell
2200 Ross Ave., Suite 2200
Dallas, TX 75201
(214) 740-8000

Shank Irwin Conant Lipshy &
  Casterline
2100 Lincoln Plaza
500 N. Akard St.
Dallas, TX 75201
(214) 720-9700

Shannon Gracey Ratliff &
  Miller
201 Main St.
Fort Worth, TX 76102
(817) 336-9333

Thompson & Knight
1700 Pacific Ave.
Dallas, TX 75201
(214) 969-1700

OIL AND GAS

Although most sectors of the state's economy are expected to post fairly large employment gains during the next fifteen years, oil and gas isn't one of them. In fact, the Texas Employment Commission officially reclassified oil and gas as a "declining industry," a dramatic signal that the Texas economy can no longer run on black gold. Now the state is busy trying to diversify its economy away from oil into more promising areas like high technology, services, and biotechnology.

That's not to say there aren't any job opportunities in the oil and gas business. There are, for enterprising people willing to risk working in an industry so vulnerable to foreign influence. But jobs will be limited as a leaner and more cautious industry emerges in the 1990s.

Opportunities for geologists and petroleum engineers are expected to remain scarce for the next few years, although some oil companies report hiring one or two on an "as needed" basis. Area career counselors say they are seeing displaced geologists changing careers and finding jobs in related fields, such as hydrology.

The local oil industry added a new player when Exxon, the world's largest oil company, decided to move its corporate headquarters from New York City to the Las Colinas development in Irving. Although Exxon has offered transfers to all 300 employees in the headquarters facility, it is expected to hire an unknown number of employees locally.

The following list includes some of the area's largest energy companies, as well as some smaller independents, in various segments of the oil and gas business.

American Petrofina Inc.
8350 N. Central Expwy.
Dallas, TX 75206
(214) 750-2400
Headquarters for oil and gas exploration, production, refining, and marketing company.

Atlantic Richfield Co.
1601 Bryan St.
Dallas, TX 75201
(214) 880-2500
Oil and gas exploration and production company.

Caltex Petroleum Corp.
125 E. John Carpenter Fwy.
Irving, TX 75062
(214) 830-1000
World headquarters for international oil exploration, production, and refining company.

Dresser Industries Inc.
1600 Pacific Ave.
Dallas, TX 75201
(214) 740-6000
Headquarters for energy-related products and services company.

Endevco Inc.
8080 N. Central Expwy., 12th
Floor, LB47
Dallas, TX 75206
(214) 691-5536
*Headquarters for natural gas
transportation company.*

Enserch Corp.
300 S. St. Paul St.
Dallas, TX 75201
(214) 651-8700
Headquarters for diversified energy, engineering, and construction company. Parent of Lone Star Gas.

Exxon Corp.
1251 Ave. of the Americas
New York, NY 10020-1198
(212) 333-1000
World's largest diversified oil company. Exxon is moving its headquarters to Las Colinas in Irving. Until the move is completed in mid-1990, direct inquiries to the New York office.

Halliburton Co.
3600 Lincoln Plaza
500 N. Akard St.
Dallas, TX 75201
(214) 978-2600
Headquarters for oil field services, engineering, and construction company.

Harken Energy Corp.
4001 Airport Fwy., 5th Floor
Bedford, TX 76021
(817) 267-1777
Headquarters for oil and gas, refining and marketing, and convenience store company.

Hunt Oil Co.
1401 Elm St.
Dallas, TX 75202-2970
(214) 744-7911
Independent oil and gas exploration and production company.

Kaneb Services Inc.
2400 Lakeside Blvd., Suite 600
Richardson, TX 75081
(214) 699-4000
Headquarters for energy services, pipeline and offshore drilling company.

LTV Corp.
Energy Products Group
2441 Forest La.
Garland, TX 75042-7928
(214) 487-3000
Headquarters for oil and gas drilling and production company and distributor of tubular goods and oil field supplies.

Maxus Energy Corp.
717 N. Harwood St.
Dallas, TX 75201
(214) 953-2000
Headquarters for major oil and gas exploration and production company. Formerly Diamond Shamrock.

Meridian Oil Co.
801 Cherry St.
Fort Worth, TX 76102
(817) 390-9200
Independent oil and gas exploration company.

Mobil Oil Corp.
1201 Main St.
Dallas, TX 75250
(214) 658-2933
Regional headquarters for major international petroleum refining and distribution company.

Oryx Energy Co.
5656 Blackwell St.
Dallas, TX 75231
(214) 890-6000
Independent oil and gas exploration company.

Snyder Oil Partners L.P.
801 Cherry St., Suite 2500
Fort Worth, TX 76102
(817) 338-4043
Oil and gas acquisition and development limited partnership.

Texas Oil & Gas Corp.
1700 Pacific Ave.
Dallas, TX 75201
(214) 954-2000

Oil and gas exploration, transmission, and marketing company. Unit of USX Corp.

Triton Energy Corp.
4925 Greenville Ave.
1400 One Energy Square
Dallas, TX 75206
(214) 691-5200
Oil and gas exploration and production company.

Union Pacific Resources Co.
801 Cherry St.
Fort Worth, TX 76102
(817) 877-6000
Petroleum exploration and production company.

Western Co. of North America
6000 Western Place
Fort Worth, TX 76107
(817) 731-5100
Headquarters for oil field services and offshore drilling contractor.

PRINT MEDIA AND PUBLISHING

Dallas–Fort Worth is a major market for print media, including newspapers, magazines, wire services, trade publications, and publishing companies. In addition to organizations that provide local coverage, several national newspapers and magazines, including *The New York Times* and *Business Week*, maintain small bureaus in the area to cover news in Texas and the Southwest.

The area is one of the most intensely competitive markets in the United States for local coverage. Dallas is one of the few remaining major U.S. cities with competing daily newspapers, *The Dallas Morning News* and the *Dallas Times Herald*, which have been waging a bitter newspaper war for years. A third major daily, the *Fort Worth Star-Telegram*, also covers the region, emphasizing Tarrant County. All three dailies maintain news bureaus in both cities. In addition, most suburbs have newspapers that cover their communities.

The print media offers jobs in a variety of areas—reporters, editors, copy editors, news artists, photographers, reference librarians, computer systems experts, advertising salespeople, and circulation and distribution staff.

Most of the major dailies, magazines, and wire services prefer applicants with several years' experience, although they do hire talented graduates straight out of college or journalism school. Several news organizations offer internships to aspiring reporters, copy editors, and advertising salespeople. See the section on internships under "Career Exploration and Training Opportunities" for more information about sponsoring organizations.

Part-time jobs are also available in the print media. Reporters without much experience are often able to break into the business in suburban newspapers or bureaus. Many publications accept free-lance work from previously published writers.

Listed below are some of the print media organizations and publishing companies in the area.

NEWSPAPERS

Carrollton Chronicle
Farmers Branch Times
Coppell Gazette
1712 Belt Line Rd.
Carrollton, TX 75011
(214) 446-0303
Weekly newspapers covering Carrollton, Farmers Branch, and Coppell.

City Life
2908 McKinney Ave.
Dallas, TX 75204
(214) 871-8901
Weekly newspaper for the central business district and surrounding area.

Dallas Business Journal
4131 N. Central Expwy.,
   Suite 310
Dallas, TX 75204
Metro (214) 263-0449 or
   (214) 520-1010
Weekly business journal.

Dallas/Fort Worth Suburban
   Newspapers
1000 Ave. H. East
Arlington, TX 76001
Metro (817) 695-0500
Chain of seven daily community newspapers covering Arlington, Garland, Grand Prairie, Irving, Mesquite, the Mid-Cities, and Richardson.

The Dallas Morning News
Communications Center
508 Young St.
Dallas, TX 75202
(214) 977-8222
Major daily newspaper with morning edition.

Dallas Observer
2330 Butler St., Suite 115
Dallas, TX 75235
(214) 637-2072
Weekly entertainment and features tabloid.

Dallas Times Herald
1101 Pacific Ave.
Dallas, TX 75202
(214) 720-6111
Major daily newspaper with morning and afternoon editions.

El Sol de Texas
4260 Spring Valley Rd.
Dallas, TX 75244
(214) 386-9120
Weekly Spanish-language newspaper.

The Business Press
501 Jones St.
Fort Worth, TX 76102
(817) 336-8300
Weekly tabloid covering Tarrant County business.

Fort Worth Star-Telegram
400 W 7th St.
Fort Worth, TX 76102
Metro (817) 429-2655
Major daily newspaper with morning and afternoon editions.

Lewisville Daily Leader
Professional Bldg., Suite 100
Lakeland Plaza
Lewisville, TX 75067
(214) 436-3566
Community newspaper published five times a week.

Park Cities People
Northside People
6116 N. Central Expwy.,
   Suite 230
Dallas, TX 75206
(214) 739-2244

Weekly community newspapers covering Highland Park and University Park and north Dallas.

Plano Star Courier
801 E. Plano Pkwy.
Plano, TX 75074
(214) 424-6565
Daily community newspaper.

The Texas Lawyer
400 S. Record St., Suite 1400
Dallas, TX 75202
(214) 744-9300
Weekly tabloid covering the legal profession.

The Wall Street Journal
1233 Regal Row
Dallas, TX 75247
(214) 631-7250
Publishes Southwest edition of The Wall Street Journal.

MAGAZINES

ADWEEK/Southwest
2909 Cole Ave., Suite 220
Dallas, TX 75204
(214) 871-9550
Weekly advertising and marketing trade publication.

American Way
4200 American Blvd.
Fort Worth, TX 76155
(817) 355-1556
In-flight magazine of American Airlines.

D Magazine
3988 N. Central Expwy.,
 Suite 1200
Dallas, TX 75204
(214) 827-5000
Monthly general interest magazine.

Dallas Life Magazine
Communications Center
508 Young St.
Dallas, TX 75202
(214) 977-8433
Weekly general interest magazine published by The Dallas Morning News.

Fort Worth Magazine
120 St. Louis Ave.
Fort Worth, TX 76104
(817) 332-6306
Monthly magazine of the Fort Worth Chamber of Commerce.

Oil & Gas Journal
4849 Greenville Ave., Suite 660
Dallas, TX 75206
(214) 739-3338
Monthly magazine for the petroleum industry.

Texas Catholic
3915 Lemmon Ave.
Dallas, TX 75219
(214) 528-8792
Weekly religious publication (biweekly in summer).

WIRE SERVICES

Associated Press
4851 LBJ Fwy., 3rd Floor
Dallas, TX 75244
(214) 991-2100

United Press International
13900 Midway Rd.
Dallas, TX 75244
(214) 980-8300

BOOK PUBLISHERS

Holt Rinehart & Winston Inc.
301 Commerce St., Suite 3700
Fort Worth, TX 76102
(817) 334-7500
Headquarters for college textbook publishing division.

Southern Methodist University
 Press
Box 415
Dallas, TX 75275
(214) 739-5959
American studies, anthropology/archaeology, ethics, film, regional folklore, regional fiction and nonfiction, Texana.

Taylor Publishing Co. Inc.
1550 W. Mockingbird La.
Dallas, TX 75235
(214) 637-2800
Yearbooks and general interest books.

Texas Christian University Press
2800 S. University Dr.
Reed Hall, Room 105
Fort Worth, TX 76109
(817) 921-7822
Texana, novels, history, general academic.

University of North Texas Press
Center for Texas Studies
P.O. Box 13016
Denton, TX 76203
(817) 565-2142

Regional fiction, nonfiction, poetry, reference, critical biography.

Wordware Publishing Inc.
1506 Capital Ave.
Plano, TX 75074
(214) 423-0090
Computer books, business and professional reference.

REAL ESTATE

"The real estate business in Dallas–Fort Worth in the next few years will be focused primarily on maximizing the value of existing assets rather than new development. That means an emphasis on asset management—assessing how assets can be repositioned to enhance their value—and property management. Another segment of the business that is likely to see a lot of activity is appraising. Frankly, I'm not sure there will be a significant enough recovery to support a dramatic number of new realtors."

Ron Witten, president, M/PF Research Inc.

The real estate industry is beginning to recover from a disastrous crash in the late 1980s, when area building activity dropped to its lowest levels of the decade. New home sales are improving slowly, but commercial developers still aren't building much in the Dallas–Fort Worth area.

Further improvement is expected as the state's population grows. The Texas Employment Commission forecasts area employment in real estate will increase by more than fourteen thousand jobs by 1995. Real estate operators, lessors, agents, and managers will account for most of the new jobs.

The bright spot in the area real estate business has been investment from outsiders. Low property values have attracted investors from out-of-state and foreign countries, particularly Japan. As a result, the area real estate market is enjoying a surge of outside investment activity that may help strengthen the recovery and bring in new jobs.

Until commercial and residential building activity picks up again, the best job opportunities in the next few years will be picking up the pieces from the crash. The most promising positions will be property managers, asset managers, and appraisers.

The following is a selective listing of area home builders, developers, property managers, and consultants and the type of properties and services they offer.

RESIDENTIAL

Centex Corp./Fox & Jacobs Inc.
3333 Lee Pkwy.
Dallas, TX 75219
(214) 559-6500
Home builder.

Coldwell Banker
4925 N. O'Connor Rd.,
  Suite 105
Irving, TX 75062
(214) 541-0900
Residential sales and leasing, relocation services.

Ebby Halliday Realtors
4455 Sigma Rd.
Dallas, TX 75244
(214) 980-6600
Residential sales and leasing, property management, relocation services.

Henry S. Miller Real Estate Co.
2001 Bryan Tower
Dallas, TX 75201
(214) 748-9171
Residential sales and leasing, relocation services.

Richmond American Homes
6200 LBJ Fwy., Suite 200
Dallas, TX 75240
(214) 490-4500
Home builder.

DIVERSIFIED DEVELOPMENT

Centre Development Co.
14001 N. Dallas Pkwy.,
  Suite 800
Dallas, TX 75240
(214) 980-8060
Office, industrial.

Herring Marathon Group
13355 Noel Rd., Suite 1200
Dallas, TX 75240-6678
(214) 458-1200
Retail.

Lincoln Property Co.
500 N. Akard St.
Dallas, TX 75201
(214) 740-3300
Commercial, multi-family.

Paragon Group Inc.
7557 Rambler Rd., Suite 1200
Dallas, TX 75231
(214) 696-8000
Commercial, multi-family.

Prentiss Properties Limited Inc.
1717 Main St., Suite 5000
Dallas, TX 75201
(214) 761-1717
Office, industrial.

Trammell Crow Co.
3500 Trammell Crow Center
2001 Ross Ave.
Dallas, TX 75201-2997
(214) 979-5100
Worldwide headquarters for one of the nation's largest developers. Also has international operations. Commercial, residential, hotels, marts, health care.

Woodbine Development Co.
1445 Ross Ave., Suite 5000
Dallas, TX 75202
(214) 855-6000
Restoration, commercial, industrial, mixed-use.

PROPERTY MANAGEMENT

Cushman & Wakefield of Texas
  Inc.
5430 LBJ Fwy., Suite 1100
Dallas, TX 75240
(214) 770-2500

LaSalle Partners Asset Management Ltd.
1201 Elm St., Suite 5210
Dallas, TX 75270
(214) 651-8808

Swearingen Management Co.
1445 Ross Ave., Suite 4300
Dallas, TX 75202
(214) 922-8700

**MARKET RESEARCH/
CONSULTING**

M/PF Research Inc.
5550 LBJ Fwy., Suite 300
Dallas, TX 75240
(214) 980-2900
*Real estate market research and
consulting firm.*

RETAILING AND WHOLESALE
MERCHANDISING

Dallas–Fort Worth is the hub of the state's retailing industry, as well as the site for what is said to be the world's largest wholesale merchandise market, the Dallas Market Center complex. The center has eight buildings totaling more than nine million square feet: the World Trade Center, the Trade Mart, Market Hall, the Apparel Mart, the Menswear Mart, the Home Furnishings Mart, the Decorative Center, and the newest addition, the Infomart computer and software mart.

Both retailing and wholesaling have been hurt by the state's weak economy in recent years. Several large retail chains consolidated, merged, or closed their doors when sales fell. The consolidation caused a mass exodus of large department stores from downtown areas in both cities. Wholesalers at the Dallas Market Center complex, in turn, have been receiving fewer orders for their goods.

Several nationally known retailers have large anchor stores at area shopping malls. These include Bloomingdale's, Saks Fifth Avenue, Macy's, and Marshall Field. The Dallas–Fort Worth area is also home base for several nationally known retailers. Specialty department store Neiman-Marcus, famous for its upscale merchandise, customer service, and the unusual items in its Christmas catalog, is based in Dallas. Dallas is also national headquarters for J. C. Penney, Michaels Stores, Sound Warehouse, and Tuesday Morning. Fort Worth is headquarters for Tandy, operator of the Radio Shack chain of computer and consumer electronics stores, and Pier 1 Imports.

Retail companies with headquarters operations offer a variety of jobs in finance, personnel, buying and merchandising, advertising and marketing, in addition to sales and management.

While retail sales are rebounding at many local stores, the job market is still tight. Thousands of workers were displaced in the consolidations and closings. Some retail employees are still looking for work and stores are more cautious about new hiring.

Some of the positions available include buyers, salespeople, public relations managers, merchandise distributors, sales promotion managers, and administrative and clerical workers.

The wholesale industry employs manufacturers' and wholesale representatives, sales reps, and showroom managers. But keep in mind that wholesalers usually don't have large staffs. Some wholesalers may have just one or two representatives working in the area.

A sample of the area's retailers and wholesalers is in the listing that follows. Food retailers are listed in the "Food and Beverage" section on page 175.

Army and Air Force Exchange
  Service
3911 S. Walton Walker Blvd.
Dallas, TX 75236
(214) 780-2011
World headquarters for domestic and overseas military retail and food service organizations.

Dallas Market Center Co.
2300 N. Stemmons Fwy.
Dallas, TX 75258
(214) 637-2171
Dallas Market Center complex owner.

Dillard's Department Stores
  Inc.
Fort Worth Division
4501 N. Beach St.
Fort Worth, TX 76137
(817) 831-5111
National department store with many area locations.

The Dunlap Co.
200 Greenleaf St.
Fort Worth, TX 76107
(817) 336-4985
Headquarters for chain of department stores throughout the state, including Stripling & Cox with several Tarrant County locations.

Foley's Department Stores
13138 Montfort Dr.
Dallas, TX 75240
(214) 385-6533
Houston-based department store with many area locations.

Home Interiors & Gifts Inc.
4550 Spring Valley Rd.
Dallas, TX 75244
(214) 386-1000
Headquarters for direct seller of decorative accessories.

Horchow
13800 Diplomat Dr.
Dallas, TX 75234
(214) 888-9700
Upscale mail-order house, division of the Neiman-Marcus Group.

K mart
701 S. Industrial Blvd.
Euless, TX 76039
Metro (817) 267-4151
National discount department store with many area locations.

Lord & Taylor
450 NorthPark Center
Dallas, TX 75225
(214) 691-6600
Specialty department store with several Dallas locations.

Mary Kay Cosmetics Inc.
8787 Stemmons Fwy.
Dallas, TX 75247
(214) 630-8787
*Headquarters for national direct
seller of cosmetics.*

Michaels Stores Inc.
5931 Campus Circle Dr.
Irving, TX 75063
(214) 580-8242
*Headquarters for specialty arts
and crafts store retail chain.*

Montgomery Ward & Co.
2700 E. Pioneer Pkwy.
Arlington, TX 76010
(817) 649-4903
*National department store with
many area locations.*

Neiman-Marcus
1618 Main St.
Dallas, TX 75201
(214) 741-6911
*Headquarters for specialty de-
partment store with several area
locations.*

J. C. Penney Co.
14840 N. Dallas Pkwy.
Dallas, TX 75240
(214) 591-1000
*National headquarters for major
department store with many area
locations.*

Pier 1 Imports
301 Commerce St., Suite 600
Fort Worth, TX 76102
(817) 878-8000
*National headquarters for retail
import store chain.*

Sears, Roebuck & Co.
Administrative Offices
5334 Ross Ave.
Dallas, TX 75206
(214) 841-2300
*National department store with
many area locations.*

Sound Warehouse Inc.
10911 Petal St.
Dallas, TX 75238
(214) 343-4700
*National headquarters for home
entertainment audio and video
software retail stores.*

The Southland Corp.
2711 N. Haskell Ave.
Dallas, TX 75204
(214) 828-2011
*National headquarters for
7-Eleven convenience stores.*

Tandy Corp.
One Tandy Center
Fort Worth, TX 76102
(817) 390-3700
*National headquarters for Radio
Shack consumer electronics re-
tail stores.*

Tandycrafts Inc.
1400 Everman Pkwy.
Fort Worth, TX 76140
(817) 551-9770
*Specialty retailer of leather
goods.*

Tuesday Morning Inc.
14621 Inwood Rd.
Dallas, TX 75244
(214) 387-3562
*National headquarters for dis-
count retail store chain.*

Westgate Fabrics Inc.
1000 Fountain Pkwy.
Grand Prairie, TX 75050
Metro (214) 647-2323
Fabric wholesaler.

Zale Corp.
901 W. Walnut Hill La.
Irving, TX 75038
(214) 580-4000
*National headquarters for retail
jewelry store chain.*

TELECOMMUNICATIONS

"We've got a core of telecommunications companies coming in here now—MCI, Fujitsu—deciding this is where they want to grow. It will be a much more effective way of doing business if all the key players are together. When that happens, you're going to have spin-offs. To people looking for a job in telecommunications, I'd say this area is the first place they ought to send their resumes."

Brian Murphy, spokesman, Northern Telecom, Inc.

If you want to work in telecommunications, the Dallas–Fort Worth area is the place to be in the 1990s. The local telecommunications industry is poised for perhaps its biggest burst of new hiring and business growth in the next few years, making it one of a handful of industries generating significant numbers of new jobs in this region.

Telecommunications giant MCI Communications is consolidating its engineering work force in Richardson. GTE is moving its telephone operations from Stamford, Connecticut, to Irving. And Fujitsu America is building a new manufacturing, research, and development complex in Richardson.

The expansions mean thousands of new jobs for people with electrical engineering, computer science, and marketing backgrounds. Although MCI and GTE are relocating many of the workers they need from other facilities, they expect to hire locally as well. Fujitsu plans to triple its area work force from about four hundred to twelve hundred by the end of 1992 and up to five thousand by the turn of the century.

In addition to Fujitsu, two other companies with Japanese roots, Uniden and NEC America, also have expanded their telecommunications operations in Dallas–Fort Worth in recent years.

The growth means new business for the existing core of local telecommunications companies. MCI is expected to buy hundeds of millions of dollars' worth of telecommunications gear from other companies in the area, including DSC Communications, Northern Telecom, Ericsson, and Fujitsu.

Even before the wave of expansions, Dallas–Fort Worth ranked as one of the country's top locations for companies that design, develop, manufacture, and market a variety of telecommunications equipment and provide telecommunications services. Local telecommunications officials rank Dallas–Fort Worth behind only San Francisco Bay's Silicon Valley and Boston's Route 128 in the concentration of telecommunications companies. Locals have already crowned the Richardson–Plano corridor the "digital switching capital of the world" because of the concentration of companies that make digital switches.

Northern Telecom's Brian Murphy, who has observed the local telecommunications business for more than a decade, says he thinks networks and cellular communications will be particularly strong specialties in coming years. Companies like Northern are looking for "knowledge workers" with computer science and electrical engineering backgrounds to develop the specialized software that differentiates telecommunications products today. Local telecommunications companies also hire heavily in marketing, sales, and customer service.

The Texas chapter of the American Electronics Association is a good source for information about telecommunications companies. The AEA's national office publishes a directory of high-technology businesses with geographic cross-references. See the section "Business Networks and Professional Organizations" for more about the AEA.

The following listing indicates the breadth of the region's telecommunications industry. Companies whose primary products are computers, electronics, or software also may be found in the "High Technology" list on page 183.

Amdahl Corp.
Communications Systems
    Division
2200 N. Greenville Ave.
Richardson, TX 75081
(214) 699-9500
Administrative office for division that manufactures integrated digital networks and data transmission multiplexing, and switching equipment.

AT&T
2777 Stemmons Fwy.,
    Suite 1425
Dallas, TX 75207
(214) 879-1800
Long-distance service, sales, maintenance, operator service, administrative functions.

AT&T Microelectronics
3000 Skyline Dr.
Mesquite, TX 75149
(214) 288-2000
Manufacturing plant for electronic power supplies used in tele-communications systems, computers, and switching and transmission equipment.

DSC Communications Corp.
1000 Coit Rd.
Plano, TX 75075
(214) 519-3000
Corporate headquarters for manufacturer of digital switching, transmission, and local network systems.

Ericsson North America Inc.
730 International Pkwy.
Richardson, TX 75081
(214) 669-9900
North American subsidiary of Swedish telecommunications company. Sales and administrative offices for Ericsson companies that develop cellular telephone equipment, central office switching equipment, and business telephone systems. Some pre-assembly work and software development.

Fujitsu America Inc.
1111 Digital Dr.
Richardson, TX 75081
(214) 699-9341

Designs and develops high-speed fiber-optic transmission systems.

GTE Corp.
290 E. John Carpenter Fwy.
Irving, TX 75062
(214) 717-7700

Headquarters for telephone operations group. Provides telephone service and publishes telephone directories.

International Telecharge Inc.
108 S. Akard St.
Dallas, TX 75202
(214) 744-0240

Provides operator-assisted long-distance services.

MCI Communications Corp.
400 International Pkwy.
Richardson, TX 75081
(214) 783-4900

Long-distance telephone service provider and headquarters for engineering operations.

Motorola Inc.
Mobile Products Division
5555 N. Beach St.
Fort Worth, TX 76137
(817) 232-6000

Manufactures two-way communications equipment.

Murata Business Systems
5560 Tennyson Pkwy.
Plano, TX 75024
(214) 403-3300

U.S. headquarters of Japanese facsimile machine manufacturer.

NEC America Inc.
1525 Walnut Hill La.
Irving, TX 75038
(214) 580-9100

Switching and business systems divisions, administration, engineering, sales, and manufacturing.

Network Access Corp.
1830 N. Greenville Ave.
Richardson, TX 75081
(214) 238-9676

Designs and develops processors for local telephone operating companies' central office switching equipment.

Northern Telecom Inc.
2100 Lakeside Bldg., Greenway Bldg.
Richardson, TX 75081
(214) 437-8000

Designs and sells corporate networking systems and designs; develops, manufactures, and sells business telecommunications systems.

Rockwell International Corp.
1200 N. Alma Rd.
Richardson, TX 75081
(214) 996-5000

Manufactures light-wave and microwave transmission systems, telephone switching equipment.

Shared Resource Exchange Inc.
17919 Waterview Pkwy.
Richardson, TX 75252-8018
(214) 907-6700

Manufactures and markets digital telecommunications switching systems for small- and medium-sized businesses.

Southwestern Bell Telephone Corp.
One Bell Plaza
P.O. Box 655521
Dallas, TX 75265-5521
(214) 464-0326

Provides local telephone service; sells telephone equipment, cellular telephone service; publishes directories through other subsidiaries. Call (214) 464-3171 for recorded list of job openings.

Teknekron Infoswitch
4401 Cambridge Rd.
Fort Worth, TX 76155
(817) 354-0661

Manufactures telecommunications switches.

Uniden Corp. of America Inc.
4700 Amon Carter Blvd.
Fort Worth, TX 76155
(817) 858-3300
*Manufactures commercial and
consumer transceivers.*

VMX Inc.
17217 Waterview Pkwy.
Dallas, TX 75252
(214) 907-3000
*Corporate headquarters for devel-
oper of voice-mail systems.*

TRANSPORTATION

The Metroplex's central geographic location in the United States and in the Southwest have made it a hub for airlines. In fact, the area's air transportation business is poised for perhaps its biggest burst of activity since Dallas/Fort Worth International Airport opened in 1974.

The new Fort Worth Alliance Airport and industrial park about fifteen miles north of downtown Fort Worth is expected to generate tens of thousands of jobs. Billed as the world's first industrial airport, Alliance will allow giant cargo planes to taxi directly into industrial tenants' factory loading docks.

Fort Worth–based American Airlines, the free world's largest airline, is also building a new maintenance facility at Alliance that will employ about forty-five hundred workers by the mid-1990s. The airline already is Fort Worth's second largest employer with twenty-one thousand area workers.

In addition, discussions are under way about expanding D/FW International, one of the country's largest and busiest air terminals. D/FW already directly employs about twenty-five thousand people, from baggage handlers to airline chief executives, and its expansion could create thousands of new jobs by the turn of the century.

Dallas, Fort Worth, and Addison also operate several municipal airports. A few carriers are talking about expanding service at Dallas Love Field, home base for Southwest Airlines.

Airports and air carriers hire many different kinds of workers with a variety of skills. The most obvious are pilots, flight attendants, mechanics, baggage handlers, and ticket and reservation agents. But air transportation also offers employment for accountants, administrators, marketing analysts, engineers, and data processing professionals.

The following list reflects the variety of transportation companies in the Dallas–Fort Worth area.

AIR TRANSPORTATION

American Airlines Inc.
4200 American Blvd.
Fort Worth, TX 76155
(817) 355-1234

National headquarters for largest airline in the free world.

Aviall Inc.
7511 Lemmon Ave.
Dallas, TX 75209
(214) 956-5000

Jet engine overhaul and maintenance.

Dallas/Fort Worth International
   Airport Board
Dallas/Fort Worth International
   Airport, TX 75261
Metro (214) 574-8888

Commercial international airport and regional air traffic control.

Delta Air Lines Inc.
8700 N. Stemmons Fwy.
Dallas, TX 75247
(214) 879-6000

Second largest airline at Dallas/ Fort Worth International Airport, employing more than five thousand locally. Has major hub at D/FW International Airport and district marketing office in Dallas.

Fort Worth Alliance Airport
c/o The Perot Group
777 Main St., Suite 1480
Fort Worth, TX 76102
(817) 877-3100

World's first industrial airport.

Metro Airlines Inc.
One Metro Center
1700 W. 20th St.
Dallas/Fort Worth International
   Airport, TX 75261-2626
Metro (214) 453-4400

Headquarters for regional airline.

Sky Chefs Inc.
601 Ryan Plaza
Arlington, TX 76011
(817) 792-2123

Headquarters for in-flight airline caterer. Food preparation facility located at D/FW International Airport.

Southwest Airlines Co.
8008 Aviation Place
Dallas, TX 75235
(214) 902-1100

National headquarters for regional airline.

RAILROADS

Burlington Northern Railroad
3800 Continental Plaza
777 Main St.
Fort Worth, TX 76102
(817) 878-2000

Headquarters for national freight railroad company.

ENTREPRENEURSHIP: WORKING FOR YOURSELF

The Dallas area is a very viable market for starting a new business. Locally, there are about fifty-seven thousand small businesses and more resources available than ever before."
> Dr. Glen Bounds, provost,
> Bill J. Priest Institute for Economic Development

Where are the jobs in Dallas–Fort Worth? You might think the majority of people worked at huge, high-profile corporations like Texas Instruments, General Dynamics, or American Airlines. Many do, but the biggest area employer isn't big at all—it's small business.

More than two thirds of all the jobs created in the metropolitan area are in companies employing fewer than a hundred workers. The North Texas Commission recently discovered that small businesses account for almost six hundred thousand area jobs—more than the top hundred employers combined. In contrast, companies with a hundred or more employees have not experienced any significant job creation and were responsible for most of the jobs lost in the economy during the four-year period the commission studied.

Much of the job growth in small business comes from new companies starting up every day. Dallas–Fort Worth is a hotbed for entrepreneurs, particularly in the high-technology industry, which is constantly spinning off new businesses. The best-known local entrepreneur is probably Ross Perot, who founded the data processing giant Electronic Data Systems with $1,000 in savings. Perot ended up selling the company

211

to General Motors for $2.5 billion—and then started another computer services company.

There are many other examples of area entrepreneurs who struck it rich with an idea. There also are lots of examples of entrepreneurs who went broke. But today there are more resources than ever in Dallas–Fort Worth to train entrepreneurs in the basics of business management, to give professional advice along the way, and to eliminate some of the obstacles that cause many small businesses to fail. Several organizations offer a range of services to start-ups and small companies—from assistance in writing a business plan to financial support.

The region is also developing more "business incubators," which typically group start-up companies and existing small businesses and give them access to shared clerical and support services and management professionals. The system increases the chances that the new business will succeed, because overhead is fixed and the companies receive guidance and advice from seasoned professionals.

In addition to the resources listed below, you should also contact your local Chamber of Commerce. Chambers frequently hold seminars on topics of interest to small business owners and entrepreneurs. They also may know of special programs in the community or in a particular industry. Many of the area's large accounting firms also have "entrepreneurial services" consulting practices aimed at small businesses that need and can afford professional help.

The following are some of the area resources for entrepreneurs and small business owners and managers.

ORGANIZATIONS

Caruth Institute for Owner-
Managed Business
Edwin L. Cox School of
Business
Southern Methodist University
Dallas, TX 75275
(214) 692-3326
Offers courses and seminars for entrepreneurs and students on how to start a business and other topics, cosponsors annual Southwest Venture Capital Conference.

Dallas–Fort Worth Minority
Business Development Center
1445 Ross Ave., Suite 800
Dallas, TX 75202
(214) 855-7373
Provides management and technical assistance to existing or emerging minority businesses. Operated by accounting firm Grant Thornton under a U.S. Commerce Department contract.

Defense Contract Administration Services Region
(DCASR)
Small Business Office
1200 Main St.
Dallas, TX 75202-4399
(214) 670-9205

Assists small and disadvantaged businesses that want to become or already are Defense Department subcontractors. Distributes list of subcontractors to industry, aids in referral, provides guidance, counseling, and information.

International Trade Resource
   Center
World Trade Center
2050 N. Stemmons Fwy.,
   Suite 150
Dallas, TX 75258
(214) 653-1113

Provides counseling, training, and educational programs and information for businesses wanting to export.

Bill J. Priest Institute for Economic Development
Dallas County Community College District
1402 Corinth St.
Dallas, TX 75215
(214) 565-5700

Small Business Development Center provides classroom instruction and guidance; job training center trains entry-level employees; Center for Government Contracting helps small businesses identify and bid on government contracts. Also operates Business Incubation Center (see below).

Small Business Administration
Dallas District Office
1100 Commerce St.,
   Room 3C36
Dallas, TX 75242
(214) 767-0605

Fort Worth office:
819 Taylor St.
Fort Worth, TX 76102
(817) 334-3777

Provides financial assistance, counseling, management assistance, seminars, and publications. Sponsors the Service Corps of Retired Executives (SCORE),

providing free consulting by volunteer retired business executives.

Southwest Venture Forum
Edwin L. Cox School of
   Business
Southern Methodist University
Dallas, TX 75275
(214) 692-3326

Nonprofit forum that holds bimonthly meetings with speakers on entrepreneurship topics and invites entrepreneurs to present business plans.

Texas Department of
   Commerce
Small Business Division
410 E. 5th St.
Austin, TX 78701
(512) 320-0110

Provides information about resources available to small businesses and start-ups, holds conferences on topics such as business incubators.

BUSINESS INCUBATORS

Advanced Technology Innovation Center
University of Texas at Dallas
2201 Waterview Dr.
Richardson, TX 75051
(214) 690-2250

Specializes in high-technology start-ups. Provides flexible space that grows with companies, guidance from seasoned professionals, access to university resources.

Bill J Priest Institute for Economic Development
Dallas County Community College District
1402 Corinth St.
Dallas, TX 75215
(214) 565-5700

Business Incubation Center is first nonprofit incubator in Dallas County. Provides start-up businesses with a place to operate in a supportive environment for one to three years.

BUSINESS NETWORKS AND PROFESSIONAL ORGANIZATIONS

Professional organizations offer excellent networking opportunities. The professional development is just as important—learning more about the industry and profession and what the different career paths are."

Julie Wilson, Fort Worth chapter of
Public Relations Society of America

One of the best ways to find a job is through personal contacts, and one of the best ways to develop such a network is to join a professional organization or a networking group.

These groups give you access to insiders in a particular field or a variety of occupations. They can help you find a job, learn more about your industry and its career paths, introduce you to industry leaders, and give you a chance to exchange ideas with peers.

In addition, many colleges and universities have alumni chapters in the Dallas–Fort Worth area. These groups are particularly good for networking, since members already have something in common and usually represent a spectrum of industries and occupations. Contact your alumni association for names of people living in the area.

The Fort Worth Chamber of Commerce publishes a listing of many associations in its directory *Clubs, Organizations and Associations in Tarrant County*. In addition, organizations that include public service in their activities can be found in the Greater Community Council of Dallas's directory of human service organizations and in the United Way of Metropolitan Tarrant County's "blue book" of community resources (see under "Libraries, Directories, and Publications" for more information about these directories).

PROFESSIONAL ORGANIZATONS

Professional organizations offer unique services that can save you a lot of time in a job search. Many publish newsletters that include notices of job openings, conduct training, or educational seminars, and maintain job hot lines and resume files—in addition to providing great networking opportunities and professional development.

Most associations charge membership dues and many have specific requirements for membership, so check with the organization you're interested in joining. Most organizations allow nonmembers to attend meetings and functions as guests.

If you're relocating to the area and are a member of a national professional organization, you can transfer your membership. If you're in college or just starting out in a particular field, some associations have student chapters at area universities or offer "associate" memberships with lower dues.

Below is a sampling of professional organizations representing some of Dallas–Fort Worth's key industries and offering job development services for members.

Advertising Club of Fort Worth
P.O. Box 18376
Fort Worth, TX 76118
(817) 283-3615
Contact: Grace Collins

For advertising, public relations, and marketing professionals, publishes monthly newsletter with free employment classified ads. Internship program available for college students.

American Electronics
  Association
Texas Chapter
800 E. Campbell Rd., Suite 254
Richardson, TX 75081
(214) 437-9222
Executive Director: Candace
  Crawford

For electronics company managers, officers, and associate members. Holds meetings and monthly small business network luncheon, publishes directory.

American Institute of Architects
Dallas Chapter
2811 McKinney Ave.
Dallas, TX 75204
(214) 871-2788

Fort Worth Chapter:
4388 W. Vickery Blvd.,
  Suite 101
Fort Worth, TX 76107
(817) 763-0242
Executive Director: Suzie
  Adams

215

Professional organization of licensed architects, affiliates, and associates. Holds monthly meetings, publishes a monthly newsletter, and maintains a resume file.

Dallas Advertising League
P.O. Box 561152
Dallas, TX 75356-1152
(214) 688-1705
Executive Director: Joan Organ

Publishes newsletter in trade publication ADWEEK/Southwest every third week. Holds regular meetings with educational speakers.

Dallas Bar Association
2101 Ross Ave.
Dallas, TX 75201
(214) 969-7066
Executive Director: JoAnna
  Moreland

For licensed attorneys. Sections and committees hold regular meetings. Publishes monthly newsletter with classified employment ads. Holds attorney resumes on file.

International Association of
  Business Communicators
Dallas Chapter
P.O. Box 2681
Dallas, TX 75221
(214) 855-5225
(214) 744-6056—Job Hot Line
President: Gayle Porter

Organization for communications professionals, free-lance artists, and writers. Holds monthly meetings, publishes monthly newsletter and free-lance directory, cosponsors recorded job line with Public Relations Society of America.

Press Club of Dallas
400 S. Houston St.
Dallas, TX 75202
(214) 748-3329
Executive Director: Mary Jane
  Hewes

Sponsors fund-raising projects, social events, and professional awards. Publishes a newsletter and provides informal job referrals.

Public Relations Society of
  America
North Texas Chapter
P.O. Box 12033
Dallas, TX 75225
(214) 350-3118
(214) 744-6056—Job Hot Line
Administrator: Kristin Gold

Organization of public relations professionals. Publishes monthly newsletter, holds meetings, special events, and seminars, cosponsors job line with International Association of Business Communicators.

Public Relations Society of
  America
Fort Worth Chapter
219 Main St.
Fort Worth, TX 76104
(817) 870-1128
Contact: Julie Wilson

Same membership requirements as north Texas chapter. Holds monthly meetings, publishes monthly newsletter with employment classified ads. Maintains a resume file. Informal mentoring program.

Tarrant County Bar Association
2015 Texas Bldg.
Fort Worth, TX 76102
(817) 338-4092

Publishes newsletter every other month with employment classified ads. Holds attorney resumes on file.

Texas Society of Certified Public Accountants
Dallas Chapter
12222 Merit Dr., Suite 300
Dallas, TX 75251-2217
(214) 960-8311

Professional organization of CPAs. Publishes newsletter, holds meetings, maintains a resume file.

Fort Worth Chapter
1701 River Run, Suite 607
Fort Worth, TX 76107
(817) 335-5055

Holds regular meetings and publishes a newsletter with employment classified ads.

WOMEN'S NETWORKING AND PROFESSIONAL ORGANIZATIONS

The list of professional organizations and networking groups aimed specifically at women continues to grow in the Dallas–Fort Worth area. Women in a variety of professions are forming their own organizations to tackle job-related issues unique to women, such as maternity leave and child care programs, opportunities for advancement in traditionally male-dominated fields, and promoting professonal development.

Women's networks are a good way to meet other career-oriented women, exchange ideas, and learn about other professions and job opportunities.

The following are some of the women's professional organizations and networking groups in the Dallas–Fort Worth area and the career development services they provide.

Association for Women
  Journalists
2333 Lotus Ave.
Fort Worth, TX 76111
(817) 831-4748
Contact: Gayle Reaves
Open to women and men in print and broadcast journalism. Holds regular meetings and networking lunches, publishes newsletter with occasional job listings.

Network for Executive Women
P.O. Box 2612
Fort Worth, TX 76113
(817) 884-5839
Contact: Pat Casey
Network of women executives, professionals, entrepreneurs, and other career-oriented women. Holds regular breakfast and dinner meetings with guest speakers.

Women in Communications
  Inc.
Dallas Professional Chapter
P.O. Box 740022
Dallas, TX 75374
(214) 350-9899
President: Sano Blocker
Organization for women in public relations, advertising, media, film, and audio/video. Holds monthly meetings, publishes newsletter, maintains job bank, conducts career conference for college students and entry-level people.

SURVIVAL
RESOURCES

Finding a job is one of the most stressful challenges in anyone's life. The search can be especially hard if you were laid off or quit your job and don't have any income to cushion you while you're looking. Another scenario is the person who left a good job in another city when a spouse relocated and now feels depressed and homesick.

The pressure can strain family relationships and pocketbooks, as well as undermine your self-confidence; but it's important to remember it's a temporary situation. You're not alone and help is available not only in financial assistance but also in emotional support and personal and employment counseling.

The Dallas–Fort Worth area has a wealth of resources for individuals and families facing short-term crises like unemployment. Several local organizations provide telephone information and referral lines to steer you to the right resource. Don't be afraid or ashamed to use them. Because of massive displacement of workers in the oil and gas, real estate, and banking industries in recent years, some social service organizations have expanded their programs. Many provide counseling and training to help build your self-confidence and revive your job search.

The following is a selective listing of some of the area organizations and services that can help you manage your transition. Nonprofit organizations and government agencies providing employment counseling are listed under "Career Information, Counseling, and Job Referral Resources."

When contacting the organizations listed below, be sure to ask about eligibility requirements. If you're eligible, take advantage of the help. The assistance can be a valuable resource to help get you through a temporary but tough time.

INFORMATION AND REFERRAL LINES

Community Council of Greater
  Dallas Inc.
2121 Main St., Suite 500
Dallas, TX 75201
(214) 741-5851 or
  1-800-548-1873

Provides information and referral to social service agencies. Publishes list of social service organizations and resources in an annual directory.

United Way of Metropolitan
  Tarrant County
First Call for Help
210 E. 9th St.
Fort Worth, TX 76102
(817) 878-0100

Provides information and referrals to social services, support groups, or community organizations in Tarrant County. Publishes list of community human services organizations in annual "blue book" directory.

FINANCIAL COUNSELING

Consumer Credit Counseling
  Service of Greater Dallas Inc.
1949 Stemmons Fwy., Suite 200
Dallas, TX 75207
(214) 748-2227

Consumer Credit Counseling
  Service of Greater Fort Worth
  Inc.
807 Texas St., Suite 100
Fort Worth, TX 76102
(817) 334-0151

Provides credit counseling to financially distressed families and individuals. Fee for debt management program. Offices throughout area.

MENTAL HEALTH INFORMATION AND REFERRAL HOT LINES

Contact Dallas
(214) 233-2233

Twenty-four-hour telephone counseling service.

Contact Telecare
Fort Worth
(817) 277-2233

Twenty-four-hour telephone counseling service.

FINANCIAL ASSISTANCE

Dallas County Department of
  Human Services
4917 Harry Hines Blvd.
Dallas, TX 75235
(214) 920-7850

Assistance to senior citizens and persons who are unemployed or have financial need. Field offices throughout the county.

Tarrant County Department of
  Human Services
3206 Miller Ave.
Fort Worth, TX 76119
(817) 531-3995

Financial assistance to residents based on need. Provides counseling, vouchers for food, rent, and utility payments, and assistance in locating other community resources for financial needs.

UNEMPLOYMENT INSURANCE

Texas Employment
  Commission
District Office
8300 John Carpenter Fwy.
Dallas, TX 75356
(214) 631-6050

Provides information about unemployment insurance eligibility, processes applications, and offers seminars and counseling. Claims offices throughout the area. See partial listing in the section "Career Information, Counseling, and Job Referral Resources."

LIBRARIES, DIRECTORIES, AND PUBLICATIONS

There are fantastic resources at libraries for researching companies. It takes a little time, but it pays off. If I've got two students applying for a job, both with good grades, and one asks intelligent questions and has obviously studied the company, I'd be biased in that applicant's favor. It shows he or she went one more step."

Bernie List, associate dean, Erik Jonsson School of Engineering and Computer Science, University of Texas at Dallas

Research is one of the most powerful tools in your job search. It can help you explore what careers and training opportunities are available, find out about particular companies and industries, make the right contacts, ask intelligent questions in an interview; it can even prevent you from making a career mistake. The information you get from research empowers you to conduct a self-directed job search and gives you the confidence to make sound career decisions.

The Dallas–Fort Worth area has a wide range of research resources for the job hunter. Libraries are stocked with career books and industry information. Many directories devoted to the Dallas–Fort Worth area or to certain industries provide comprehensive listings and information about potential employers. Area newspapers and magazines are also good sources for news and features about local businesses and employment trends.

To maximize your research, take advantage of all three resources. Much of the information is free through area libraries. All it costs is time.

LIBRARIES

The Dallas–Fort Worth area has dozens of public libraries and branches; in addition, there are many college and university libraries that let the public use their reference materials.

The central public libraries in downtown Dallas and Fort Worth both have separate business and technology sections loaded with industry directories, local business publications, and business periodicals and journals. Both libraries have *Contacts Influential*, a comprehensive listing of area companies, on microfiche. They also have 10K annual reports from almost every public U.S. company on microfiche. Books on a range of business and career topics can also be checked out.

City libraries have branches throughout the area, but check with their reference departments to see if they have the types of books you're looking for.

Most area college and university libraries are open to the public for research, although you can't check out any materials. On their shelves you'll find many books, periodicals, and directories useful for job hunting. College libraries are particularly good sources for highly specialized subjects in which they have academic programs.

Listed below are the main area libraries and one of the best specialty libraries.

Dallas Public Library
Business and Technology
  Section
5th Floor
1515 S. Young St. at Ervay St.
Dallas, TX 75201
(214) 670-1700

Fort Worth Public Library
Business and Technology
  Section
300 Taylor St.
Fort Worth, TX 76102
(817) 870-7701

Southern Methodist University
Science and Engineering
  Library
6425 Airline Rd.
Dallas, TX 75275
(214) 692-2282
Reference materials available to public, but you must be a student to check out books.

DIRECTORIES

Directories are one of the most useful tools for identifying the companies and organizations where you may want to work. Usually directories provide valuable information such as addresses, names of officers and directors (potential contacts), descriptions of products and services, employment figures, and even financial data.

A variety of general business directories are available, listing companies, nonprofit groups, and social service organizations, as well as directories devoted to a specific industry such as oil and gas or banking. Some directories are too expensive to buy yourself. Local public libraries have copies of most of them in their business reference departments.

The Dallas and Fort Worth Chambers of Commerce publish several good business directories, including a membership and buyers guide and a directory of leading employers in each city. Other community Chambers throughout the area also publish membership directories and business guides.

Below is a selective listing of some especially good directories.

*Community Council of Greater
  Dallas Directory of Services*
2121 Main St., Suite 500
Dallas, TX 75201
(214) 741-5851
*Community services and non-
profit organizations listed with
names of administrators, descriptions of services, eligibility
guidelines, fees, hours of operation, and funding sources.*

Contacts Influential
1250 E. Copeland Rd.,
  Suite 800
Arlington, TX 76011
(817) 543-5000
*Annual publications with Dallas
and Tarrant County editions.
Lists area companies alphabeti-
cally by name or by industry,
with information on principal officers, number of employees, and
products and services. The Dallas
and Fort Worth central downtown libraries have the publications on microfiche.*

*Directory of Foreign-Owned
Firms in Dallas–Fort Worth*
Dallas Chamber of Commerce
1201 Elm St., Suite 2000
Dallas, TX 75270
(214) 746-6600

*Foreign-owned companies by
year of local establishment, products and services, and area
employment.*

*Directory of Texas
  Manufacturers*
Bureau of Business Research
University of Texas at Austin
P.O. Box 7459
Austin, TX 78713
*Manufacturers with sales data,
names of officials, and descrip-
tion of work.*

First Call for Help
United Way of Metropolitan
  Tarrant County
210 E. 9th St.
Fort Worth, TX 76102
(817) 878-0100
*Community service and nonprofit
organizations, with names of administrators, description of services provided, eligibility
guidelines, fees, hours of operation, and funding sources.*

*Greater Dallas Business and In-
  dustry Guide*
Dallas Chamber of Commerce
1201 Elm St., Suite 2000
Dallas, TX 75270
(214) 746-6600
*Top two hundred Dallas firms
ranked by employment.*

223

*Major Employers in Fort Worth
and Tarrant County*
Fort Worth Chamber of
Commerce
777 Taylor St., Suite 900
Fort Worth, TX 76102
(817) 336-2491
*Annual publication listing public
and private companies in Fort
Worth and Tarrant County with
a hundred employees or more.*

Rotan Mosle Guide
Scholl Communications Inc.
P.O. Box 560
Deerfield, IL 60015
(312) 945-1891
*List of publicly held companies
and financial institutions in
Texas and Oklahoma, with description of operations, officers
and directories, and financial
data.*

*The Sibbald Guide to the Texas
Top Two-Fifty*
The Durham Group
561-K Acorn St.
Deer Park, NY 11729
(516) 254-4840

*Profiles of the state's top 250
public and private companies
and financial institutions.*

Texas Banking Red Book
Bankers Digest Inc.
6440 N. Central Expy.,
Suite 215
Dallas, TX 75206-4103
(214) 373-4544
*Annual listing of financial insti-
tutions with names of key executives and financial information.*

Texas Savings & Loan Directory
Texas State Directory Press
P.O. Box 12186
Austin, TX 78711
(512) 477-5698
*Annual listing of S&Ls with
names of key executives and fi-
nancial information.*

U.S.A. Oil Industry Directory
Penn Well Publications
P.O. Box 21288
Tulsa, OK 74101
(918) 835-3161
*National directory of oil compa-
nies, independents, marketing
companies, and associations
with geographical index.*

PUBLICATIONS

Publications that cover business are valuable to the job
hunter because they report news that may affect a company
or organization's employment or financial outlook, put industry trends in perspective, and often profile local businesses.

The area's three major daily newspapers also publish Help
Wanted sections that could turn up some job leads and let
you see which companies and industries are hiring and which
jobs are in most demand. The best day to scan the classifieds
is Sunday, when the local papers group the employment ads
in a special, stand-alone section indexed by key industries.

Newspapers, magazines, trade journals, and newsletters
are all good sources of business information. Dallas–Fort
Worth's three major daily newspapers all have stand-alone
business sections and large classified advertising sections that
break employment ads into industry categories. Smaller sub-

urban newspapers are also devoting more coverage to business, economics, and employment news. In addition, several weeklies devoted to business coverage provide more news and features, as well as regular rankings and lists of businesses.

General interest magazines in the area also frequently report on business trends and trade publications provide an insider's view of a particular industry or occupation. Local libraries subscribe to many trade publications and journals.

Listed below are some of the publications covering business and employment topics and a newsletter that follows the federal employment scene.

The Business Press
501 Jones St.
Fort Worth, TX 76102
(817) 336-8300
Weekly tabloid covering Tarrant County business, with analysis, trend stories, profiles, and rankings of local companies.

Dallas Business Journal
4131 North Central Expy.,
    Suite 310
Dallas, TX 75204
Metro (214) 263-0449 or
    (214) 520-1010
Weekly business publication with news, features, and periodic rankings of top twenty-five Dallas businesses in various categories. Compiles rankings in annual Book of Lists.

The Dallas Morning News
Communications Center
508 Young St.
Dallas, TX 75202
(214) 977-8222
Dallas's leading daily newspaper, with morning editions. Separate daily business section. Publishes annual Scorecard, tabloid ranking top public and private companies. Expanded business section every Tuesday.

Dallas/Fort Worth Suburban
    Newspapers
1000 Ave. H East
Arlington, TX 76001
Metro (817) 695-0500
Chain of seven daily community newspapers in Arlington, Gar-
land, Grand Prairie, Irving, Mesquite, the Mid-Cities, and Richardson. Regularly covers business topics of interest to the community.

Dallas Times Herald
1101 Pacific Ave.
Dallas, TX 75202
(214) 720-6111
Major Dallas daily newspaper with morning and afternoon editions. Separate daily business section, special Dallas, Inc. business report on Sunday with features and profiles of area businesses.

Federal Employment Bulletin
Federal Job Information
    Services
P.O. Box 121505
Arlington, TX 76012
(817) 261-5257
Publishes newsletter with information about how to apply for federal jobs and list of federal job openings in Texas and the Southwest.

Fort Worth Star-Telegram
400 W. 7th St.
Fort Worth, TX 76102
Metro (817) 429-2655
Fort Worth's leading newspaper, with morning and afternoon editions. Separate daily business section. Publishes Tarrant County Business tabloid every Monday, with news, features, and rankings of area businesses.

Plano Star Courier
801 E. Plano Pkwy.
Plano, TX 75074
(214) 424-6565

*Daily community newspaper
with news and profiles of local
businesses.*

The Wall Street Journal
Southwest Edition
1233 Regal Row
Dallas, TX 75247
(214) 631-7250

*National business newspaper
published weekdays. Dallas bureau produces news stories and
features about publicly held area
companies.*

SUGGESTED READING

Allen, Jeffrey G. *Surviving Corporate Downsizing: How to Keep Your Job*. New York: John Wiley & Sons, 1988.

Figler, Howard E. *The Complete Job Search Handbook*. Rev. and expanded ed. New York: Owl Books, 1988.

Irish, Richard K. *Go Hire Yourself an Employer*. 3rd ed. New York: Anchor Press/Doubleday, 1987.

Ivantcho, Barbara. *A Selected Annotated Bibliography on Work Time Options*. San Francisco: New Ways to Work Publications, 1987.

Krannich, Ronald L., Ph.D., and Krannich, Caryl Rae, Ph.D. *Network Your Way to Job and Career Success*. Manassass, Virginia: Impact Publications, 1989.

Parker, Yana. *The Resume Catalog: 200 Damn Good Examples*. Berkeley, California: Ten Speed Press, 1988.

Scheele, Adele. *Skills for Success*. New York: Ballantine Books, 1981.

Sher, Barbara, and Gottlieb, Annie. *Wishcraft: How to Get What You Really Want*. New York: Ballantine Books, 1987.

Simon, Dr. Sidney B. *Getting Unstuck: Breaking Through Your Barriers to Change*. New York: Warner Books, 1988.

Sinetar, Marsha. *Do What You Love, the Money Will Follow*. Mahwah, New Jersey: Paulist Press, 1987.

ABOUT THE AUTHORS

Barbara Block and Janice Benjamin combine over twenty years of career counseling experience with advanced academic credentials. Ms. Block is the founder and past president of the Career Management Center in Kansas City, Missouri, and now lives in Tiburon, California, where she is a free-lance business writer and columnist. Ms. Benjamin, the current president of the Center, lives in Kansas City, where she counsels individuals and consults with employers on career and work issues.

Kathryn Jones is a business reporter and staff writer on the *Dallas Morning News*.